CYRIL WILD

The Tall Man Who Never Slept
nemuranu se no takai otoko

JAMES BRADLEY

Jim Bradley
3.12.91.

W
Woodfield

By the same author:

Towards the Setting Sun, an escape from the Thailand – Burma Railway, 1943.

First published in 1991 by

WOODFIELD PUBLISHING
Woodfield House, Arundel Road, Fontwell,
West Sussex BN18 0SD, England.

British Library Cataloguing in Publication Data

Bradley, James *1911 –*
   Cyril Wild: the tall man who never slept.
   1. Great Britain. Japan. World War 2, prisoners of war.
   I. Title.
   940.547252092

   ISBN 1 – 873203 – 20 – 9

And a voice valedictory. . . . Who is for Victory?
Who is for Liberty? Who goes home?

Who Goes Home?
G.K. Chesterton

CONTENTS

ILLUSTRATIONS
(See section between pages 80 & 81)

1. David and Cyril in 1912
2. Patrick, Cyril, John and David, 1916
3. The Bishop and his four sons, 1927
4. Mount Nantai-San, Lake Chūzenji, Nikko, Japan
5. Cyril fishing the Kisugawa river, Chūzenji, 1931
6. Cyril and his best man, David, 1935
7. Cyril and Celia – their marriage, 1935
8. Allied Surrender – Cyril carrying white flag – 15 February 1942
9. Japanese Surrender – Singapore ceremony – 12 September 1945
10. Christian crosses over 'Chinese graves' – Cyril and Koshirō Mikizawa, commandant of Outram Road Gaol, 1945
11. Cyril in his office at Singapore during war crimes investigations, 1946
12. Interrogation of Major-General Kojima – Cyril and Lt-Col Henry Haynes, 1946
13. Cyril in the witness box at the Tokyo Tribunal, 11 September 1946
14. The Very Revd John Wild holding General Yamashita's sword, October 1988
15. (& 16) The Union Jack, with dedication, now in Charterhouse chapel, 1989

MAPS

FOREWORD

I am sure my father, had he still been alive, would have been pleased to write a Foreword to this account of the amazing deeds of one of the officers serving with him in South-East Asia, whom he knew personally, when he was Supreme Allied Commander during and after the famous Burma Campaign.

Major Cyril Wild was a man after my father's own heart; a born leader, fearless in battle, resolute against terrible adversity and able to communicate with a wide variety of people.

But I am sure it would have been Major Wild's heroic defence of his fellow prisoners-of-war in Japanese camps, often at great personal cost, against the inhuman treatment and brutality meted out to them, that would have meant most to my father. During the terrible conditions of that campaign nothing remained graven on his heart like the suffering endured – so often until death – of the men fighting under his command when taken prisoner, whom he was powerless to help, except by speeding up the victorious campaign as much as was humanly possible. He felt this horror deeply to the end of his days.

Major Wild's story would be quite unbelievable, were it not absolutely true. Alas this suffering was also endured with great stoicism and heroism by many thousands of our prisoners. But Major Wild was one of their real champions and managed to save the lives and alleviate the suffering of many. Above all, his dauntless bravery and leadership shone out as a beacon of light and hope in the blackest of worlds.

It is tragic that Cyril Wild's life was ended so soon after the war, after a brief glimpse of personal happiness that was to be denied to him even after all he had endured, and with a bright future ahead. At least he had the satisfaction of being instrumental in bringing many of his, and other prisoners' tormentors to justice.

Perhaps his best testimonial is the name by which the Japanese called him – "The Tall Man Who Never Slept" – telling of his devotion to his fellow prisoners.

MOUNTBATTEN OF BURMA

INTRODUCTORY NOTE

This book is not so much a biography as a piecing-together of Cyril Wild's life in, as much as possible, his own words – written and spoken. I have quoted liberally, believing this to be the best way of bringing his personality to life and, since Cyril was a classical scholar with a great love of literature, I had no wish to change his carefully chosen phrases, which portray so clearly his charm and vitality. This could not have been done without the generosity and encouragement of Cyril's two surviving brothers, the Very Reverend John Wild and the Reverend David Wild, MBE, MC, who unhesitatingly put at my disposal all their letters, articles, reports and photographs. I am particularly grateful to David for casting his mind back to childhood years, thus providing much of the material for the first chapter.

Cyril's verbatim testimony at the Tokyo War Crimes Tribunal has, until recently, remained closed to the public under the 30-year rule. However, thanks to Roderick Suddaby and Philip Reed of the Department of Documents at the Imperial War Museum, who made available to me the relevant volumes, I hope I have been able to extract a readable précis from the many hundreds of pages. Although war crimes work took up only the last year of Cyril's life, his contribution historically to the outcome of the trials was significant and warrants the two chapters devoted to them.

In his supporting document to Colonel Harris's *Recommendation for Award*, General Percival added the note that, 'The Japanese called Cyril "the tall man who never slept".' This refers to his unceasing efforts on behalf of his fellow men and his availability at all times.

Countess Mountbatten has very kindly written the foreword to my book, and this in itself is a further tribute to Cyril. I am most grateful to her.

Above all I want to thank my wife, Lindy, who not only typed the text several times, never having overcome her fear of being 'taken over' by a wordprocessor, but also helped with research and in the construction and writing of the book. We did it together, and both feel extremely privileged to have been entrusted with the absorbing task of compiling this record of Cyril Wild's life, as a tribute to his selfless work during those dark years.

JIM BRADLEY
Midhurst, Sussex
February 1991

N.B. Where Japanese names appear I have put the given name before the surname, Western style.

Notes are listed at the end of each chapter.

ACKNOWLEDGMENTS

Apart from the key people I have already thanked in my introductory note I would like to acknowledge the help given to me so willingly by the following:

Canon James Mansel, KCVO, for the loan of letters; Mrs. Juliet Wood (née Piggott), Major-General F.J.C. Piggott, Lady Rawlings and Mrs. Mary Beazley for reminiscences; Geoffrey Pharaoh Adams for the loan of photographs and documents; Eric Lomax for helpful references; Dr. Hank Nelson of The Research School of Pacific Studies, Australian National University, also for references; Dr. John Pritchard for information on war crimes; Major-General M.D. Price, CB, OBE, for permission to quote from his article in Journal of the Royal Signals Institution 1981; Mrs. A.C. Wheeler, Charterhouse Librarian, for her enthusiastic research in the Charterhouse archives; and Tim Bradley, our Carthusian son, for his help with research and photographs.

Finally, I want to make special mention of the help given to me by the late Ewart Escritt, OBE. Although he didn't know Cyril Wild personally, he was himself a prisoner-of-war of the Japanese, and a great authority on the war in the Far-East. He was also a translator of the Japanese language, a scholar and a perfectionist where the written word was concerned. It was to him that I always turned for advice on accuracy, and in his meticulous way he took the time and trouble to proof-read my typescript, for which I am immensely grateful. Sadly, he did not live to see this book in print.

Chapter 1
EARLY LIFE 1908 – 1930

Cyril Hew Dalrymple Wild was born on 10 April 1908 at his grand-
mother's house in Earls Court Square, London. He was the third son
of Herbert Louis Wild, at that time Vicar of St John's Carrington,
Nottingham, and his wife, Helen Christian (née Severn). He was to
have another brother and a sister, all five children being born at Earls
Court Square.

In 1909, when Cyril was one, the family moved to Oxford, a
city already familiar to Dr Wild: not only was he a scholar of Exeter
College and later an Honorary Fellow, but he had for eight years been
Vice-Principal and Chaplain of St Edmund Hall. He now became Vicar
of St Giles, the church where Cyril was later to marry. In 1913 he was
appointed Rector of Southwell and Archdeacon of Nottingham, and two
years later was consecrated Bishop of Newcastle. He was a scholar, an
impressive, able and friendly man with a true pastoral sense, a good
diocesan bishop. Unfortunately he never really recovered his health
after suffering in the devastating influenza epidemic of 1918, and he
later developed Parkinson's Disease which led to his retirement in 1927.
Hard work and increasing infirmity over the years rendered him less and
less accessible to his young family and, though he followed their progress
with affection and concern, communication was never easy.

His wife Christian was the only daughter of Walter Severn, the
half-artist, half-civil servant son of Joseph Severn, the artist friend
of Keats. Her uncle, Arthur and her aunt, Mary Severn, were also
distinguished artists. Her mother was Mary Fergusson, daughter of Sir
Charles Dalrymple Fergusson, Bart, of Kilkerran in Ayrshire. Christian
was a delightful person. She gave devoted support to her husband in his
professional life and later in his long illness, and both at Newcastle and
in retirement at Oxford she effortlessly kept open house for innumerable
guests, many of them the young friends of all five of her children. She
lived, in fact, so much for others that it left her little time to develop
her considerable inherited talent as a painter in water-colour. Her own
faintly Bohemian home in London had also given her a lifelong love of

1

literature, music and the theatre, interests all reflected in Cyril's letters from Japan in the 1930s.

As in many clerical homes of those days, with large houses and extensive gardens, the Wild children – John, Patrick, Cyril, David and Rose Mary – were able to pursue freely their interests and amusements. Cyril was a 'dreamy' child and would bury himself in books for hours on end. He was a voracious reader of romantic tales, Henty, Scott, and the writers of heroic poetry and this was reflected in imaginative games about knights in armour, Red Indians and so on, in which he would involve his not always cooperative younger brother and sister. Most of the encounters so devised ended in fights to the finish with Cyril always the triumphant but magnanimous victor. He was to retain this interest in books and literature throughout his short life, and he had a deep love of poetry.

His serious education began with a governess at Southwell. When he reached preparatory school age at Newcastle he did not immediately join his two elder brothers at boarding-school, Summer Fields at Oxford. Instead he travelled daily by tram to a day school the other side of Newcastle. When, at the age of eleven, he finally went to Summer Fields he had ground to make up scholastically and it was not until the middle of his time at Charterhouse, his father's old school to which Patrick had preceded him, that his real ability became apparent. He entered the school in 1921 at the age of thirteen, and in House (Robinites) photographs he is seen to be a tall, slender boy with sharply-defined features in an alert and sensitive face. His literary flair revealed itself in due course; he was runner-up for the Thackeray prize for English Literature and was awarded a Holford Exhibition. He sat on the Library and Debating Society Committees, and a Debating Society report in *The Carthusian* of 7 November 1926 is an interesting forerunner of things to come:

'That this house considers capital punishment a bad thing.' In proposing this motion C.H.D. Wild pointed out that civilisation as it advanced had seen the lessening of the number of crimes for which death was the penalty. Capital punishment was a relic of the past which was incompatible with civilisation.

I wonder if he still held this view when he acted as Liaison Officer on the War Crimes Commission after the end of the war.

Cyril was not a great team sportsman, as records of House cricket matches show, but he had the determination and build for cross-country running and was on the Athletics Committee. He enjoyed being a member of the school fire brigade that, in those days, boasted an archaic hand-drawn and hand-operated pump. He displayed leadership as an under-officer in the OTC during his last two terms, and also as Head of House and School Monitor.

Year after year for a summer holiday the Wild family migrated *en masse* to the West Highlands of Scotland. There, for a month, the family crammed themselves into a tiny manse at Kinlochmoidart. On Sundays the Bishop conducted services which all the family attended, providing nearly half the congregation, but on weekdays all members of the family, whatever the weather, took themselves off to fish, at first with worm in small streams and later in the many hill lochs. No member of the family was more strenuous or adventurous than Cyril in reaching the most inaccessible lochs and none more successful with the rod. His lifelong love of fishing dated from these idyllic holidays. These lines of Robert Louis Stevenson were later noted down by him in a small book of his favourite quotations:

> An angler is an important piece of river scenery... his quiet presence seems to accentuate the solitude and stillness, and remind you of the glittering citizens below your boat.

In October 1927 Cyril went up to Brasenose College, Oxford, to read Classical Honour Moderations, hoping to gain an Honours Degree in four years. Coincidentally during that summer the family returned to Oxford after the Bishop resigned his episcopal see of Newcastle. They came to live at 11 Bradmore Road which was to remain the family home until Mrs Wild's death in 1942.

At the end of his second year at Brasenose Cyril was elected President of the Junior Common Room. To his brother David, thanking him for his congratulations, he wrote:

> It was a most thrilling election between five candidates (the first contested election in living memory). The first and second year men on the whole voted for me, and the older men for the chief of the rival candidates; but that is all to the good, because my supporters will be the seniors of my year of office and my opponents will have gone down. It took a deal of resolution to stand for the post, since I feared that I would either be defeated with ignominy or elected by a fictitious majority of dim men, and that in either case I would incur the wrath of the Olympians. But in the end I received quite a representative support and everyone was very pleasant about it.

In the same letter he wrote:

> . . . Tomorrow I and three other highwaymen are waylaying the Tallyho coach at High Wycombe; the family horse-pistol lies beside me as I write.

But more of this from John, who takes up the story:

> During Cyril's time at Oxford the Tallyho coach and horses ran between
> Oxford and High Wycombe. Cyril decided that he would be a highwayman,
> so having obtained a horse he sat, suitably attired, up on the slopes of the
> Chilterns, from where he could see the road running from Oxford. As the
> coach approached he rode out dramatically and forced the coachman to
> stop. He was still the romantic, with a good sense of fun.
>
> Years later, in the short time that he was at home after the war, he told
> us of an occasion when they were talking in the prison camp one evening.
> The conversation turned to some of their crazier acts before the war, and
> Cyril mentioned his highwayman escapade. Strangely enough, one of those
> present remembered it well.

At Oxford Cyril's career overlapped that of all his three brothers. They
were to follow the example of their father and grandfather and enter Holy
Orders. John was to become Master of University College, Oxford, and
later Dean of Durham. Patrick, after service in the war as Chaplain to the
Forces, was for 30 years Vicar of Theydon Bois and became an Honorary
Canon of Chelmsford Cathedral. David was taken prisoner as Chaplain
to the 4th Batallion, Oxfordshire and Buckinghamshire Light Infantry,
at Dunkirk and, having continued his ministry for five years in prison
camps, subsequently returned as Chaplain and Housemaster to Eton
where he had been a King's Scholar. Cyril was to follow a different
course. He never achieved his Honours Degree. After five terms he
should have taken Honour Moderations in March 1929, but he was ill
and unable to sit for it. Brasenose College awarded him an exhibition
and he took the prelim. at the end of the summer term. During the long
vacation that summer he was offered a job with the Rising Sun Petroleum
Company, a subsidiary of Shell, having an introduction through Sir Claud
Severn, his uncle, who was a friend of the Chairman of Royal Dutch
Petroleum. He decided, therefore, to take a B A Pass Degree, comprising
four different subjects, and this he achieved in just one year, thanks to
his good brain and determination. According to David, 'Cyril was more
ambitious than any other Wild', and John describes him as 'dedicated,
thorough and determined'.

In July of that year Cyril joined the 4th (Territorial) Battalion
of the Oxfordshire and Buckinghamshire Light Infantry. While on
attachment for instruction with the 1st Battalion in the Isle of Wight
he wrote to David:

> I have been having a very good time here at Brook Camp. The camp
> is situated on the edge of the cliffs, with woods at the side and a fine
> view of hills inland – altogether a jolly place. It is miles from anywhere,

and the 43rd are the only troops here. I travelled down from Oxford last Saturday with Jack Tawney on a free 1st class return-ticket, which unfortunately prohibited me from taking an instrument (large), go-cart or perambulator! The British Army (esp. officers) amuses me intensely – a hard-bitten Colonel with crinkles round the eyes, a purple Major with a black moustache, a whole bevy of Captains looking like Uncle Wilfrid and several perfect subalterns. Nothing but shop and racing is discussed, and for most of the time the officers slumber in the ante-room or idly turn the leaves of antiquated *Tatlers*. But for all that it is extraordinarily good fun; the weather has been perfect and the bathing good.

Satis. I must go and bathe.

Your affectionate brother,

Cyril

After Cyril came down from Oxford in the summer of 1930 he and David, who had also joined the 4th Battalion, attended one annual camp together. Cyril then joined Shell in their City office near Liverpool Street, where he remained for one year before moving to their subsidiary, The Rising Sun Petroleum Company (also known as The Asiatic Petroleum Company), in Yokohama, Japan.

A close friendship over the years had developed in Oxford between the Wild family and the Waterhouse family. Dr Waterhouse was a well-known Oxford physician, the son of Alfred Waterhouse, the architect. His sister was married to the Poet Laureate, Robert Bridges. Mrs Waterhouse was one of the Gamlen family and her father, and later her brother, were senior partners of Morrell, Peel and Gamlen, Solicitors to the University. They had two sons and two daughters, contemporaries and close friends of the younger Wilds. For Cyril and the younger daughter, Celia, it was more than just friendship and before Cyril left for Japan they announced their engagement. They were both very young and Celia's father was against an early marriage until Cyril had an assured income, for at 23 he was barely established in his career. Dr and Mrs Waterhouse were, in fact, hesitant about Celia marrying at all because, sadly, she had only one kidney, owing to TB, and was thus unable to have children. Nevertheless, undeterred and knowing their own hearts and minds, Cyril and Celia looked ahead to a long engagement, half the world apart.

Chapter 2
JAPAN 1931 – 1940

Cyril sailed for Japan in the summer of 1931 with, I imagine, very mixed feelings and emotions. He was leaving Celia and the security of Oxford and his family for a completely new life in a country where the language, culture, customs and traditions would be totally alien to him. At the same time, it was a challenge and an adventure to which he was looking forward.

Cyril enjoyed life wherever he was, and was good at adapting to his environment. However, he found his first accommodation in a Company house in Nagoya a little hard to accept, and he wrote to David:

> I've lately inspected the sanitary equipment of this house, and how the last manager and wife brought up a baby here from the word go to the staggering stage without it dying, and why there's been nothing worse than two cases of diphtheria in the house during the last six months, passes my comprehension. I've had a strong application sent to the Company for the sinking of a septic tank, but I doubt if they'll do it. You see there are no drains at all in Nagoya. Each house has a box opening out onto the street, and now and then the municipal cart comes round in the daytime and empties it. The contents of the carts are then spread over the paddyfields, from which the sixty-seven millions of Japan derive their staple article of diet. They patriotically (and appropriately) designate this refuse "homeproduced", as opposed to imported or artificial, manure. In Tokyo, however, they are much more up-to-date, for there they have drains. But these discharge into the land-locked Bay of Tokyo, from which are drawn the fish and shellfish with which the population of the capital flavours its rice, gathered from the above-mentioned paddy-fields. And then they wonder why typhoid is so prevalent! *Dai Nippon!*

This primitive and somewhat unsanitary existence in Nagoya was, fortunately, only temporary as The Rising Sun Petroleum Company's office in Yokohama was Cyril's permanent base. (It is extraordinary to reflect how far Japan has advanced in the last fifty years, from the antiquated conditions of the thirties to the efficiency and prosperity of the eighties and nineties.)

The letter to David concludes:

Japanese notices in English are comic sometimes. Here's one which is displayed in a tailor's shop in Nagoya: "We Give Ladies Fits Upstairs". And, still better, who runs can read this, writ large across the wall of what corresponds to Jenning's Gold Medal Bakery: "The Biggest Loafer in Tokyo".

I'm finishing this on Sunday. Heape's away, and Le May seems to be spending the day in bed, so I'm left to my own devices. Nothing for it but a solitary walk in the arid foothills, and as it's 3 o'clock I'd better be moving. Rather a grim way of spending Sunday. Write again soon, it's damned lonely here sometimes.

Your affectionate brother,

Cyril

After his spartan lodgings in Nagoya Cyril moved to the greater comfort of the Yokohama United Club. Even here he must have felt very much alone and, inevitably, resorted to books to fill his leisure hours. He asked David to send out his copies of Homer and Virgil, and he kept an immaculate notebook in which he wrote, in his small neat handwriting, passages from books and poems that impressed him.

However, it was typical of Cyril to set about getting to grips with this situation. He wanted to be able to converse with the Japanese people and to understand their culture and mentality; by so doing he would not only enrich himself, but would also advance his career and prospects with Shell. He realised fully the complexities of the language, but set himself the task of learning it. In the early thirties trade began to fall off, so he took the opportunity of engaging a teacher every day in his lunch hour, and worked on his own in the evenings, making considerable progress. But it was a lonely period of his life when he missed Celia and all those at home.

After four years in Yokohama Cyril returned to England for his first leave, arriving on 8 August 1935. At last he and Celia could plan and look forward to their wedding, and decided it should take place on 9 November of that year.

In October, following a visit to David, who was doing his first curacy at Eastleigh, he went up to Oxford to take his MA. In a letter to his brother he wrote:

It was a desperate rush returning to Oxford, and on the open road I had to proceed at 45/50 m.p.h. all the way. This was too much for the car, and the distributor went phut again near the top of Boar's

7

Hill, but for which mishap I should have homed in 1 hr 50 mins. With your black trousers fluttering over one arm, and your coat and waistcoat trailing across the other, I rushed after another car and cadged a lift to the nearest taxi-stand. So I was able to take my MA after all.

Two days later, 25 October, Celia also wrote to David saying how glad she was that he had consented to be Cyril's best man:

> . . . I hope the flask won't often be wanted. Anyhow, see that he isn't all droopy by the time I arrive. I hope you will enjoy the fatal day. I hope to get a certain kick out of it myself.

Cyril's marriage was very much a family affair, with nearly everyone taking part in the ceremony. This was the report in the local paper the following week:

> The wedding took place at St Giles' Church, Oxford, on Saturday of Mr Cyril Hew Dalrymple Wild, third son of Bishop H.L. Wild, formerly Bishop of Newcastle, and Mrs Wild, of 11 Bradmore Road, Oxford, and Miss Celia Mary Waterhouse, younger daughter of Dr and Mrs A.T. Waterhouse, of 35 Beaumont Street, Oxford.
>
> Bishop Wild officiated, assisted by Canon C.C. Inge, Vicar of St Giles (David's future father-in-law), and the Revd J.H.S. Wild, Fellow of University College, who is a brother of the bridegroom. The organist was Mr H. Wilsdon and the best man was the Revd R.D.F. Wild, brother of the bridegroom.
>
> The bride wore a parchment-coloured satin beauté dress, with a draped bodice and train cut in one with the skirt. The veil, edged with old Limerick lace, was lent by her mother. She carried a bouquet of lilies.
>
> The bridesmaids were Miss Ann Waterhouse (Celia's sister) and Miss Rose Mary Wild, who wore picture dresses of bronze-red velvet, with gold wreaths in their hair, and carried red chrysanthemums.
>
> The reception was held at 35 Beaumont Street. The honeymoon is taking the form of a motor tour.

Cyril returned to Yokohama in January 1936, this time accompanied by Celia, a much happier person embarking on married life. During the few months they spent in Yokohama they found life pleasant enough, though somewhat shallow, their rather too close neighbours' main interest and conversations centring on their Chinese tailors and the next cocktail party. Celia found the climate humid, but anything was better than Oxford! They enjoyed playing the piano and singing together in the evenings, and David sent music out to them.

In July Cyril was advised to undergo an operation for the removal of the septum from his nose, which had been troubling him for some time, and he was admitted to the Yokohama General Hospital early in August.

On 10 July of that year Cyril signed the lease of a Japanese house they had found in Tokyo, very small but adequate for the two of them and one servant. The company recognised his ability to learn the language and decided to give him a year off, on full pay, in order to become fluent. They, therefore, left Yokohama to live in Tokyo, and this proved to be a very happy time for them both.

During his five years in Japan Cyril had already made friends at the British Embassy, many of whom owned or rented cottages outside Tokyo on Lake Chūzenji. It was a delightful spot, affording good trout fishing, sailing and bathing and was a favourite holiday retreat for the Embassy staff and their friends. High up in the mountains 100 miles north of Tokyo, near Nikkō, Chūzenji was a small village bordering a lake at the foot of Mount Nantai-San. The outflow from the lake cascaded down a series of beautiful waterfalls into the Kisugawa river, and there was a saying: 'Never say *kekkō* (splendid) until you have seen Nikkō'. The small yacht club at the lake was named after the mountain, the Nantai-San Yacht Club, and most of the Embassy and Service members owned and raced enthusiastically in the one-design Lark class, a centre-board dinghy.

Cyril claimed that he was a poor correspondent, but when he did write his letters were much more than mere transmissions of news. They were beautifully worded and composed; he was a perfectionist, and many of his letters contained deletions and substitutions in his search for the most apt terminology and phraseology. Of his three brothers Cyril was closest to David, being nearer in age, and most of the surviving letters were written to him.

Tokyo 24 October 1936

Dear David,

I am afraid that I still rank as a very poor correspondent, but I must write – even a short letter – to say how very much I enjoy your letters, and how much I should miss them if my shortcomings caused the fount of inspiration to run dry. And I do hope to be a more regular correspondent in future.

My nasal op. went off extremely well. The Japanese, Kurosu, who performed, was absolutely first-rate, and I felt practically no pain at the time and, what I am sure was, the minimum of discomfort afterwards. We went to Chūzenji while I was recuperating, and we enjoyed ourselves there to the full. We spent the first three nights with Geoffrey and Mimi Harrison in their delightful little Japanese cottage at the head of the lake. And the next week we spent with the Naval Attaché and Mrs Rawlings in their house on the shore of the lake. I had a yacht at my disposal and sailed with fair success in several races. The fishing was not very good, but I managed to catch two rainbow-trout of just under 1 lb. each, besides a fair number of smaller ones.

Mary Beazley, daughter of the late Naval Attaché and Lady Rawlings, writes:

> I remember Cyril surprisingly well, and the overriding memory is of an extremely nice person. This long held impression must prove, I think, that if he could be bothered to be kind to a noisy girl of eleven, then he truly was a most kind and charming man.

The Rawlings family owned three Larks, so it was probably one of these that Cyril sailed during the week that he and Celia spent with them. They had two neighbouring holiday houses on the edge of the lake, as they were quite a large family and liked to be able to entertain their friends.

Mary's memory 'is persistent in seeing Cyril as very tall, with a serious and attentive air, although I remember his smile and a very pleasant, deep voice. I feel sure that my mother and father were really very attached to the young couple, as they were then, back in the thirties.'

Lady Rawlings, at 90 years of age, writes:

> The Wilds were a delightful young couple, and we much enjoyed their visit to us at Chūzenji. We did a lot of sailing and there was a nice trout stream running into the lake. My husband was a keen fisherman, and I am sure he would have taken Cyril fishing! Cyril was very good at playing with my children, and I have a clear recollection of his arranging the funeral of a mouse! The children had some tame mice and one died. I can well remember Cyril pacing along the shores of Lake Chūzenji, carrying a very small box, containing a very small dead mouse, and intoning in true parsonical manner!

Cyril's letter to David continued:

> On our return to Yokohama I handed over my job to my successor, and severed my connection with commerce – except in connection with the pay-roll – for a year! We are now living in a small Japanese house in a very pleasant part of Tokyo. The moat of the Imperial Palace is at the bottom of our road: the War Office, Foreign Office, etc. and the magnificent new Diet Building are all within a few hundred yards, and the British Embassy Compound is close behind us. Incidentally, if we had been here last February we should have been in the centre of the rebels' position during that deplorable affair,[1] which was, however, ended with remarkable firmness and astonishingly little bloodshed – particularly in comparison with this ghastly Spanish business. (Spanish Civil War)
>
> I go to school for four hours a day to learn the language, and in addition have a good deal of work to do at home. It is a peculiarly complicated tongue, but I do enjoy trying to learn it. . .

Celia keeps herself fully occupied with Madrigals, Orchestra, Flower Arrangement. . . Also she is singing a duet and playing in the orchestra in the Tokyo ADC's production of "As You Like It", in which I shall be taking the part of the exiled Duke. The performances are to be on 20 and 21 November in the magnificent theatre of Waseda University. Ashley Clarke, the producer, who is 2nd Secretary at the Embassy (later became British Ambassador in Rome), has obtained the designs for the clothes from the Stratford Memorial Theatre, so we shall be well dressed, however indifferently we may act!

Celia's letters were effervescent, written exactly as she would have spoken. Perhaps, now and again, her mind ran ahead of her pen, resulting in the occasional missing word. In December 1936 she wrote to David:

I am overcome with horror when I realise that I have not yet said thank-you for the songs which you sent us. When I think of it I go all pink and blotchy and feel more miserable than words can say, and wish I could forget all about it. Anyway, they were exactly what we wanted, and thank you awfully for taking so much trouble. They are a great boon, and it is lovely to be able to sing Tyneside songs in Tokyo. Now that Cyril has had the inside of his nose carved out, he sings much better again, and we have both joined a madrigal-club run by a peculiar Japanese, which Cyril is learning sight-reading on, so to speak. It's quite fun.

Has Cyril told you what a success "As You Like It" was? It really was quite amazingly good for an amateur show. Ashley Clarke is so good at getting the best out of people, and we all enjoyed doing it terrifically. Cyril made a very good Duke, and looked v. handsome in purple. Everyone admired his voice very much. All I had to do was sing a duet with another female – "It was a lover and a lass". . .

It is great fun living in Tokyo. We are incredibly happy and don't in the least mind life being a picnic, which it is bound to be in a Japanese house. There is no hot tap in the house, no system in the way of pipes, and you have to go through the drawing-room to get to the bathroom, and anyway there is only a layer of paper and one of glass between us and the cold outside world. But that is where the numerous travelling-rugs we were given as wedding-presents come in. We sleep on them, and later are prepared to sleep under them as well.

The weather in the autumn is simply marvellous. Every day we wake up and look out of the window to see the sun shining red on the pine-trees and the roofs, and the sky bright blue. And by 11 a.m. the sun is always really quite hot, and the weather stays like this for weeks on end. Give me the Japanese climate any day rather than the English; to begin with because the sun is really warm even in December, January and February; in the summer it is very hot – even on grey days a cotton frock is essential, and I like the semi-tropical touches.

People are so much nicer here than in Yokohama – all really very friendly disposed, and they take an interest in things, which is such a blessing.

Cyril has gone down to Yokohama for a meeting this-evening, and goodness knows when he will be back. It is quite an hour's drive, along the most deadly of all roads. . .

By the way, I discovered a rather amazing thing this-morning. Cyril asked me to send a telegram to a man called Caiger, to say he couldn't play squash today, as he was going to Yokohama – I had the cook in, and said I wanted her to send a telegram. I got as far as saying that, "as Cyril was going to Yokohama" – and there I got a bit stuck, as I couldn't at the moment remember the present tense of the verb "to meet". Then, to my amazement, she asked if the friend was Caiger *San*, and I said it was. And she went on to say, if you please, "Oh, Danna *San* (the master) was going to play squash with him this-afternoon, wasn't he, and now he has to put him off as he is going to Yokohama, isn't that what you want to say?"

Well, she can't understand English, of that I am sure. The squash plans were fixed verbally in the bank, where Cyril and Caiger met, and till this-morning I myself didn't know of the plans. The only explanation is, and you may not believe it, but if you lived here you would, is that the police called when we were out, asked the usual questions, went up to Cyril's room to rummage through his papers and found his little Oxford University diary, and he and Kaku *San* went through that together. That sort of thing makes me furious, but Cyril doesn't mind any more. . .

Love from Celia

A very happy Christmas to you. I am afraid this will arrive much too late tho'. I am so frightfully (??) to hear of your new appointment to be private what-not to the Bishop of Winchester. It is most excellent news, and how glad you must be. Many congratulations! (David had been invited to be chaplain to the Bishop of Winchester.)

This saga of the Japanese cook knowing all about Cyril's squash game plans illustrates the xenophobia that existed in Japan at that time. Cyril and Celia both felt that, as foreigners, they were always being spied on by the servants, whom they believed were paid for information, and this constant surveillance increased in 1938/39.

In a letter to Patrick, his elder brother and fellow Old Carthusian, now ordained and living in Westminster, Cyril wrote in April 1937:

. . . I am going to recover a little lost ground by sending you a book called *Celebrated Carthusians*, in the hope that some day you will put the name of Wild on the pages of a later edition. . .

I am working very hard at Japanese these days – the reading as well as the speaking. It is a brute of a language, but I am really quite enjoying my studies, and they are a pleasant change from business. Our army, navy and air-force language-officers, and the Embassy students, all have three years for the task, and I have only one; so I have a fearful lot to cram in, although I cannot even hope to read the newspapers after one year. For that one requires a knowledge of between two and three thousand characters and I shall be doing well if I know one thousand by the end of this year.

Major-General Francis Stewart Gilderoy Piggott was Military Attaché to HM Embassy, Tokyo, at that time, 1936 – 1939, and worked hard for a better understanding between Japan and Great Britain, with the hope of preventing Japan entering the war as an ally of Germany. General and Mrs Piggott became fond of Cyril and Celia during their year in Tokyo and the General, a fluent Japanese speaker, helped Cyril with his studies in an informal capacity. (It was he who was later to use his influence to help Cyril leave Japan to rejoin his regiment.) They too had a cottage on Lake Chūzenji, near the Naval Attaché and Mrs Rawlings, and their daughter, Juliet, then aged 12, remembers sailing their Lark on the lake. Too old for military service, General Piggott later became Senior Lecturer in Japanese at the School of African and Oriental Studies in London from 1942 to 1946.

The letter to Patrick continues:

We greatly enjoy our life in Tokyo. There are any number of pleasant people to meet, both foreigners and Japanese, and lots of interesting things to do. Celia used to play in a small Japanese orchestra until recently, and they gave quite a good concert last month. Also we both sing weekly in the Tokyo Madrigal Club, which is run by a Japanese and contains three other "foreign" members besides ourselves – six altogether. We are giving a concert next week after a Japan-British Society Dinner, when we shall doubtless have Royalty present among our distinguished audience! So, as you can imagine, I am very busy learning my part. Talking of Royalty, I had the honour of being invited to a tea-party given by Prince and Princess Chichibu just before they left for England. I had quite a long talk with the Prince, who was greatly looking forward to revisiting Oxford. I owed this invitation to my position as Hon. Sec. of the Cambridge & Oxford Society in Tokyo, which has a membership of eighty, of which more than half are Japanese, including the Prince, who regularly attends our dinners. Our next one will be in the nature of a farewell to the Ambassador, who is being transferred to Brussels. I have been given the somewhat arduous task of composing a speech for the aged Marquis Kuroda, the *Daimyō* (War Lord) of Fukuoka, who will propose his health. I know now what it feels like to write a sermon, though even you have not yet, I imagine, been called on to produce one for delivery by a foreign prelate, which is about what this amounts to!

I hope that all goes well with you. With love from us both,

Your affectionate brother, Cyril

After finishing his language course in Tokyo Cyril was posted to The Rising Sun Petroleum Company's office in Osaka, and commuted there daily from Kyōto. The seemingly endless war against China was putting an economic strain on the country, and business was slack. Cyril wrote to David in June 1938, on Company notepaper, a most interesting letter giving a very clear account of conditions prevailing at that time:

My dear David,

They tell me that you and Mary (daughter of Canon Inge, who assisted at Cyril's wedding) are thinking of getting married in August. That is marvellous news, for like us you have had a very long time to wait. . .

Life out here has been pretty trying for the last nine months or so, and we have been through two particularly bad times, one at the end of last year when the anti-British feeling was at its height, with rabid articles in the vernacular press every day, and Chastise Outrageous England meetings all over the country, and the other at the time of the Anschluss. On both occasions it looked as though these people were on the point of starting something, and the prospect of being chopped in covert was most unpleasant, in fact I was seriously considering the advisability of sending Celia home on one occasion.

They don't love us any more now, but at least the press has piped down, except for the continual childish spy-scares; and I think that their hands are quite full enough in China at the moment without starting anything else. The latest sensation in our local Japanese paper was an exhortation to the citizens of Kyōto to beware of the increased spying by foreign residents and tourists: practically every tourist was held to be suspect and the future slogan of every citizen was to be, "See a foreigner and recognize a spy"! A thoroughly good idea for a city which derives a large part of its revenue from tourists! A couple of days later the Women of Kyōto were warned against the nefarious designs of the foreign residents. As I am the only foreign businessman here, and practically everyone else is a missionary or teacher, this seemed a little pointed! It has been fairly clear all along that the attacks on Britain have been intended to distract the people's attention from the slow progress in China. It has certainly had the result of making things very uncomfortable for British people living in Japan, and one will not forget in a hurry the many damnable things that have been said and written about our country and about ourselves. Things are a little better now, but it would be thoroughly nasty if the Chinese retaliated by dropping a few bombs on one of these paper and match-wood cities, or if the Russians started in and did the same. However,it is no good worrying about these things in advance. I am afraid that it will be a very long time before any permanent settlement is reached in China, and the economic strain on this country is terrific. So far the Japanese have kept things going remarkably well at home, but as far as my Company is concerned our petrol trade is now about $2/3$ of normal, owing to the rationing of consumption, and some of our other products are disappearing altogether on account of the virtual prohibition of imports. Soon we may have nothing at all to sell except a limited quantity of petrol and heavy oil. Food is still plentiful, but the cost of living is rising all the time. One has to admire the fortitude and unity of the Japanese people, whatever one's opinion may be of the terrible goings-on in China.[2]

I am always extremely busy, leaving the house for Osaka daily at 7.30 a.m. and generally not returning until 5.30 or 6.00 or later. On top of which I have Japanese to learn and another examination in prospect next August. Also I have been making a special study of the first foreign intercourse with Japan in the 16th and 17th centuries. I have amassed a lot of interesting material on the subject and I am now putting it together in the form of a book, which I hope to finish before the autumn...

This book, entitled *Purchas His Pilgrimes in Japan*, was published in Kōbe, Japan, in 1939 and, as General Piggott commented, 'showed real erudition and scholarship'. It needs some explanation. Samuel Purchas lived from 1577 to 1626 and was a compiler of travel and discovery writings. He continued the encyclopaedic collections begun by British geographer, Richard Haklyat in *Hacklytus Posthumus*, or *Purchas his Pilgrimes*. During a time when travel literature had the patriotic purpose of inspiring Englishmen to engage in overseas expansion and enterprise, his collections were read with enthusiasm, being frequently the only source of information on important questions relating to geographical history and early exploration. Nearly two centuries after it was first published *Purchas his Pilgrimes* was the favourite reading of Samuel Taylor Coleridge. On the flyleaf of Cyril's book are the words:

> *Purchas His Pilgrimes in Japan* extracted from *Hakluytus Posthumus*
> or *Purchas His Pilgrimes Contayning a History of the World*
> *in Sea Voyages and Lande Travells by Englishmen and Others*
> By Samuel Purchas, B.D.
> and edited with commentary and notes by Cyril Wild

Cyril wrote his last letter from Japan at the Kōbe Club on 14 September 1939, completely frustrated by the lack of any instructions concerning his future and his inability to return home to his Unit:

Dear David

I am longing to hear news of you and of Maurice. (Both in the Ox. and Bucks LI, David and Maurice Waterhouse, Celia's brother, had been called up on 3 September 1939.) I suddenly came across your photographs in a 4th Bn group in *The Tatler* in this Club, and I have arranged for it to be given to me later on. I suppose that the Bn is doing intensive training now, and I wish that I was with you both in it. You probably know that I am on the Reserve myself. With my knowledge of the lingo I'd have been shot out of this country, probably to Uncle Claud's old home (Hong Kong) in quick time if things had turned out as expected, but as this place is definitely going to stay neutral I have had no such luck. So far only ex-Regulars and RNR men have been called from here, and today there is an official consular announcement in the paper to the effect that all who have volunteered, and there have been many, are to stay here and carry on with their ordinary jobs, this being "in the best interests of the country, which has ample supplies of men nearer home". The Ambassador in China has apparently given similar instructions; and two men in Yokohama who resigned from their jobs, with the intention of going home to enlist, were actually ordered back to work by the Consul!

This is a big change from the last time and no doubt it's a good thing, as it shows that the authorities have matters properly organised; for everyone I know filled in National Service forms months ago. But having fixed up a quick getaway for myself ages ago I feel extremely disappointed. The worst of it is that I have almost literally nothing to do in the office – there is about half a day's work for one man, and three of us available to do it, and the prospect of weeks of enforced idleness and waiting for orders is pretty trying. However, I have hopes, as my commission must put me about top of the list, and the Company has said that it is in touch with the authorities as to which men can be spared – obviously I qualify – and where they can be of most use. Also I myself am in touch with the Military Attaché in Tokyo (General Piggott). So I hope I shall get news soon.

Certainly it would be downright folly, in face of these instructions, to chuck up my job and come tearing home, before I know where I'm wanted. But all the same, I wish I could join you and Maurice! Please give him my love, and tell him that I'll write soon. Let me know about Nickie too: we have an idea that he's a gunner. (Nicholas Waterhouse, Celia's other brother, was killed later in the war.)

There is an extraordinary change in our position here since Hitler put across a fast one by making friends with Stalin. Russia is the real enemy and chief threat to this country, so the Japanese were wild with rage. All anti-British propaganda stopped overnight, and we English out here had a really good laugh after all these months of tension. Actually there had been very amusing aspects of the anti-B. agitation, and I for one never took it very seriously – it was so obviously engineered. But "face" is of the greatest importance all over the East, and if ever anyone "lost face" it was the Japanese when Hitler double-crossed them without one word of warning. There is now not the slightest risk that Japan will join forces with Germany, in fact we may yet have them as allies if Russia does so. That possibility again might keep me here – but I wish they'd tell me something definite.[3]

I expect you feel as I do that we did all that we could, and perhaps more than we should, to avoid war, but that Hitler and all that he stands for made it inevitable. Certainly there is no hope for a better and saner world till Hitlerism is smashed, which will teach a much needed lesson to these people too. But I see the grimness of it all the more clearly for having been in a country at war for the last two years.

We had a very happy time at Chūzenji and I caught quite a lot of fish. Shioja is perfect these days and Celia and I enjoy the tennis and swimming. It is still hot, but in a week or so we shall have the glorious weather of a Japanese autumn.

16

Well, David, the best of luck to you and to Maurice, and our love to Mary. I hope still that we may all meet again soon, though it will not be quite the leave to which we were looking forward, starting 5 months from today!

Your affectionate brother,

Cyril

It was, in fact, more than six years before Cyril and David were to meet again.

Cyril sent Celia home as soon as passage could be arranged after the outbreak of war, as he was so uncertain of the future. He then turned to General Piggott to ask for help in persuading the oil company to release him, and it was through his influence and the personal intervention of General Sir George Macdonogh that he was able to rejoin his regiment in June 1940. Some men might have been content to remain in a safe and comfortable post, for eighteen months were to elapse before the start of the Pacific War, but Cyril was determined on a course of action that he thought in the greater interest of his country.

His return was marred by sadness. His father had died two months earlier and he found that David and his brother-in-law, Maurice Waterhouse, were missing. Mary will never forget the day that Cyril came to see her that summer; they had a long talk, and he told her that he felt sure David was all right. 'Because he was Cyril I believed him. It gave me a terrific lift.' (Both David and Maurice had been captured at Dunkirk in May and were to be held as prisoners-of-war for the next five years.) Cyril found that Patrick was in hospital, badly shell-shocked, and his sister, Rose Mary, desperately ill with TB, having been in various sanatoria in England, Switzerland and Denmark for the last three years. (John, who visited her in Denmark in the new year of 1939, tells of his dismay in finding that 'so many of the patients were of student age'.) Cyril was just in time to see Rose Mary before she died at the end of June, aged 27.

Mrs Wild, Cyril's mother, was to die in February 1942, surely of a broken heart, having had so much family sadness in the previous two years. Her husband and daughter were both dead, her two younger sons were prisoners-of-war on opposite sides of the world, and Patrick had been very badly shell-shocked. Fortunately, being in good health, she was able to attend Patrick's wedding in Belfast two weeks before she died. From that time Celia and Mary lived in the family house at 11 Bradmore Road, for they both had jobs in Oxford.

To return to 1940: on rejoining the Ox. and Bucks Light Infantry, Cyril was posted to a battalion serving in Northern Ireland, and was able to take Celia with him, but it was not many months before the War Office discovered his knowledge of Japanese and the fact that he had passed his final exams in Japan. Realising his potential as an intelligence officer and interpreter in the Far-East, he was posted to Singapore on the staff of General Sir Lewis Heath, the Commander of 3rd Indian Corps, with the rank of captain, and arrived out there in November 1940.

He wrote later: 'It *was* sad coming away, but Celia and I were very lucky to have all that time together in Oxford and then in Ireland, and some very happy days at Sherwood' (the Waterhouse family home) '. . . we have a good many very happy years to look back on and no *definite* period of "sentence" before us.'

NOTES

[1] Early in 1936 antagonism to the repressive economic measures of Finance Minister Takahashi Korekiyo had been growing, and this feeling reached a high point in February, when the military rose in rebellion in Tokyo. Korekiyo, whose fiscal policies had set Japan on a road to recovery after the slump of 1929/30, was killed, and thus opposition to further inflationary spending died with him.

[2] The Sino-Japanese war, disastrous for the economies of both nations, started as a minor clash near Peking on 7 July 1937 between Japanese and Chinese troops, which perhaps could have been settled locally had it not been for China's fiercely nationalistic pride. Japan at least tried to keep it as an isolated incident, but failed, and finally both nations became locked in war. Japan quickly took Peking and Tientsin, and fighting spread to Shanghai in August.

Japan, although far superior in the air and on the sea, could not commit her entire strength against China because of her wariness of Russia and America, but she continued to gain important victories. By December 1937 Shanghai was completely occupied, and Nanking had fallen with the frightful slaughter of 40,000 civilians – men, women and children.

China, with her massive manpower, made it difficult to control occupied zones, and thus the war dragged on with no further successes to hearten the Japanese nation.

[3] Hindsight makes it very easy to query this assessment of the Japanese position at that time, but undoubtedly this must have been a true reflection of the thoughts of British businessmen resident in Japan, as evidenced by the complete change of heart of the Japanese government and people towards us.

MALAYA

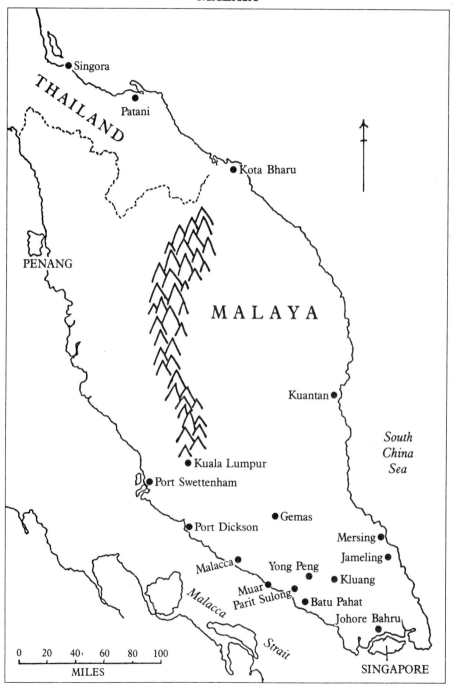

THAILAND

Singora

Patani

Kota Bharu

PENANG

MALAYA

Kuantan

Kuala Lumpur

Port Swettenham

South
China
Sea

Gemas

Port Dickson

Mersing

Jameling

Malacca

Yong Peng

Kluang

Muar
Parit Sulong

Batu Pahat

Malacca

Johore Bahru

Strait

0   20   40   60   80   100

MILES

SINGAPORE

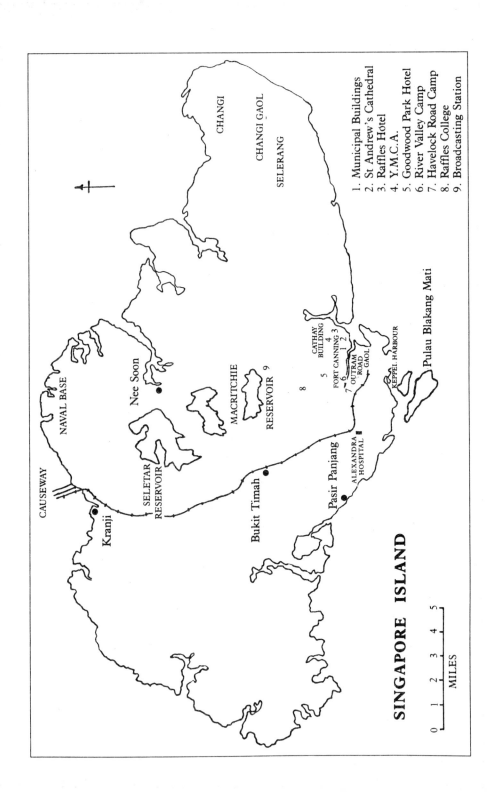

SINGAPORE ISLAND

1. Municipal Buildings
2. St Andrew's Cathedral
3. Raffles Hotel
4. Y.M.C.A.
5. Goodwood Park Hotel
6. River Valley Camp
7. Havelock Road Camp
8. Raffles College
9. Broadcasting Station

0 1 2 3 4 5
MILES

Chapter 3

MALAYA AND SINGAPORE

In June 1940 we stood alone after the German thrust through France to the Channel ports and the evacuation from Dunkirk, with the immense loss of military equipment. We were ill-prepared to repel, what seemed at that time to be, an imminent invasion. The American Ambassador, Joseph Kennedy, had little faith in our ability to survive and must have warned President Franklin D. Roosevelt of his forebodings. Winston Churchill knew that our only chance of ultimate success lay with the United States, but Roosevelt had his own problems with the Republican party who were opposed to America's entering the war against Germany.

To pursue the war on our own we needed all the resources of the Empire, which necessitated keeping open long lines of communication from Australia, New Zealand and Malaya via Singapore, the Suez Canal and the Mediterranean.

The Malay States were the world's main suppliers of rubber and tin ore, and the Dutch East Indies had vast reserves of oil, so this part of South-East Asia was obviously a target for expansion for Japan, who had little in the way of natural resources of her own.

To protect these commodities Singapore was vital, but by late 1940 Winston Churchill knew it would be impossible to hold the fortress if Japan should attack. Germany had broken the Royal Navy fleet codes and had intercepted mail from MI6 to their Far Eastern stations. Japan now knew our intended strategy and was able to plan her own expansionist policy over the next twelve months.

No serious defence strategy had ever been planned in the past, as it had always been thought that Malaya and Singapore could be defended almost entirely by the Royal Navy, and thus the construction of the Naval Base had commenced in 1922. On the outbreak of war, however, no fleet could be spared for this particular theatre and so the major responsibility had to rest with the Royal Air Force. Being an independent service there was little cooperation with the army, with the result that new airfields were sited in areas difficult to defend.

In November 1940 General Headquarters Far-East was formed, with Air Vice-Marshal Brooke-Popham as Commander-in-Chief. He estimated that to repulse any hostile seaborne attack he would need, at the very minimum, 370 modern aircraft – fighters, bombers and torpedo carriers. Most existing airfields were incapable of accommodating high-performance planes, and so a costly restructuring operation was put in hand, together with the building of entirely new airfields.

As soon as Lieutenant-General A.E. Percival assumed command he realised how woefully inadequate his land forces were, and put in a strong request for reinforcements:

(a) Third Indian Corps to be enlarged to three full divisions.

(b) The Two Australian brigades to be made up to a complete division.

(c) A full division for GHQ defence.

(d) Another division for the defence of Singapore Island.

(e) A tank regiment, with limited size tanks, as most bridges on the mainland had a very low weight-bearing capacity.

The predominant geographical feature of the Malay Peninsula was the range of mountains stretching from north to south, averaging 4,000 feet in height, with peaks reaching 7,000 feet. This completely bisected the country and, being almost entirely covered in jungle, made communications between troops on the east and the west side extremely difficult. In places the jungle was impenetrable, giving impossible fields of fire for small arms, and most rivers were too narrow to provide any natural line of defence.

Had his demands been met, General Percival was confident that he could repel any Japanese attack, but this was not to be; Malaya was starved of resources, so badly needed in the Middle East and by Russia. The planes delivered made up the total to little more than half of the 370 requested, most of which were obsolete Wildebeasts, Swordfish, and Brewster Buffaloes long since discarded by the US Air Force. (It was not until the convoy carrying 53rd Brigade, 18th Division, docked on 13 January bringing 51 Hurricanes that the RAF possessed any modern fighters, but many of these were destroyed on the ground before even taking off.)

This was the situation pertaining when Cyril was posted to 3rd Indian Corps on Lieutenant-General Sir Lewis Heath's staff in November 1940. The dictates of Whitehall were that Malaya's prime function in the war was to earn dollars by the production of tin and rubber, and great efforts were made to increase the output of these two commodities.

In October 1941 Cyril wrote home to his mother-in-law, telling her that his work as Senior Intelligence Officer was interesting and varied, and that he was pleased to have 'avoided being sidetracked as just an interpreter'. With his great ambition to succeed, he took lessons in Malay before breakfast, conversed in Japanese in the evenings, and whenever possible tried to gain some knowledge of Urdu.

He had already formed a great admiration for his commanding officer and felt himself privileged to serve under so great a soldier. He was made GSO3 at the end of September 1941. He said in the letter: 'I have really been very lucky, and I love the work.' He dined with General Heath at this time and met his newly-wed wife, who was formerly a nursing-sister in India. (Lady Heath was later interned in Changi Gaol, Singapore for three and a half years.)

In Kuala Lumpur Cyril was the only officer not in the Indian Army, but six members of the Rising Sun Petroleum Company, whom he had known in Japan, were also serving in Malaya. Being a staff officer, he missed his old regiment and the personal contact with other ranks, for whom he always had the greatest respect. There were, however, two officers of the Ox. and Bucks Light Infantry out there, both very distinguished. One was Brigadier Paris and the other was Air Vice-Marshal Sir Robert Brooke-Popham, originally commissioned in the Oxfordshire Light Infantry before transferring to the Royal Flying Corps on its formation in 1912.

He ended his letter by saying:

> I like this place very much. I am sure it must be the best station in Malaya, and the climate is quite good. I play a good deal of squash and tennis with my brother-officers, and there is a good swimming-pool at one of the clubs. We have an excellent office-building, and the mess and officers' quarters are long wooden palmleaf-roofed huts standing in the grounds, on brick piles, to keep out the white ants. My room is 7 ft × 14 ft and looks like a potting-shed from inside, but it does very well.

On 2 December 1941 HMS *Prince of Wales* and HMS *Repulse* were secured alongside in the Naval Base, having been sent by Winston Churchill as a propaganda fleet. 'Z Force', as these capital ships and their attendant destroyers were known, had no air cover as the new carrier, HMS *Indomitable*, had run aground on 3 November when working up in the Caribbean, and no other carrier was available.

In the early days of that month the trails of high-flying planes were seen over the northern airfields of Malaya, and it had to be assumed that these were Japanese reconnaissance flights. It was then obvious that an attack on the mainland was imminent, and this was confirmed on 6 December when one of our reconnoitering Hudsons sighted a large convoy of forty transports, with a strong naval escort, south of Indo-China steaming due west. This course pointed to a landing in southern Siam, close to the border with Malaya. Unfortunately, contact was lost and two long-distance Catalinas, sent out from Singapore, never returned. A similar convoy on the same course was reported 24 hours astern.

In the early morning of 8 December Japanese bombers made their first attack on the city of Singapore, and news came through of the devastating attack on the American fleet in Pearl Harbour the previous day. For the third time this century Japan had embarked on hostilities with no declaration of war, and war had now come to the Far-East. Three landings were achieved by the Japanese forces at Singora and Patani in Siam, and Kota Bahru in northern Malaya. An operation codenamed 'Matador' had been considered to counter any Japanese strike on Siam, but this would have involved the 11th Indian Division crossing into Siam before any actual landing of enemy troops in that country. Air Vice-Marshal Brooke-Popham never allowed 'Matador' to go ahead, as contact had been lost with the main Japanese convoy, and there was insufficient evidence that the first assault would be in Siam. It was considered, therefore, inadvisable to violate her neutrality.

Prince of Wales and *Repulse* immediately put to sea with their four destroyers, *Electra*, *Express*, *Vampire* and *Tenedos*, steaming on a north-easterly course, but soon received a signal from Combined HQ that the promised fighter protection would not be available. Vice-Admiral Sir Tom Phillips could not remain inactive, and really had no option but to carry on with his plan to prevent further reinforcement of the enemy troops already ashore. However, he soon received a second signal to proceed south-west, as there was the probability of further hostile landings at Kuantan. It was then that Z Force came under heavy attack from bombers and torpedo-launching aircraft. *Repulse* was hit first, but her battle efficiency remained unimpaired. *Prince of Wales* was less fortunate, as her steering was damaged and her speed reduced to about 10 knots. Both fought bravely, but eventually went down with all guns firing, after five torpedoes found their mark on each ship.

Meanwhile, the landings in Siam were almost unopposed, and that country capitulated after two hours. Siamese police, with the help of Japanese advisers, immediately started to seek out and arrest all British specialists and civilians. At Kota Bahru the Japanese achieved a successful bridgehead, in spite of the north-west monsoon blowing at the time and the fierce seas breaking along the northern shores of Malaya. By 11 December the enemy forces already landed amounted to three divisions.

Japanese dive-bombers and fighters were already operating from airfields in Siam, and fighting became confused as communications with forward troops was virtually destroyed. Under the weight of this fierce onslaught, backed by tanks and complete air superiority, our troops were forced to fall back. A feature of the whole campaign was the brilliant work of the Japanese engineers and the speed with which they effected the crossing of rivers where bridges had been totally destroyed. Time and again the enemy was helped by its fifth column, which had been secretly spying for years. Members had been working throughout Malaya and Singapore as rubber planters, hairdressers, shopkeepers and photographers.

When Penang was evacuated twenty-four motor launches and other small craft had been, surprisingly, left behind intact. These were used repeatedly to outflank our forces on the west coast and, indeed, this encircling movement was equally successful on land.

On 6 January 1942 Supreme Commander General Sir Archibald Wavell visited Command HQ and it was decided to hold a line north of Batu Pahat, Kluang and Jameling airfields on the general line of the Muar River. Here the Japanese threw in a fresh Guards division, inflicting heavy damage, but it was still hoped to hold this position. Once again it became untenable, due to the complete enemy dominance in the air, and a further outflanking movement resulted in Batu Pahat being cut off, although two thousand of our troops were evacuated by sea. The possibility of retaining a bridgehead in Johore Bahru was turned down, as the water supply could not be defended, and it was thus decided to make a general withdrawal to Singapore Island on 8 February.

As a result of a cable from Winston Churchill, General Wavell issued the following Order of the Day on 10 February 1942, which was immediately transmitted to lower echelons by General Percival:

It is certain that our troops on Singapore Island outnumber any Japanese that have crossed the Straits. We must destroy them. Our whole fighting reputation is at stake, and the honour of the British Empire. The Americans have held in the Bataan Peninsular against far heavier odds; the Russians are turning back the picked strength of the Germans; the Chinese, with an almost complete lack of modern equipment, have held the Japanese for four and a half years. It will be disgraceful if we yield our boasted fortress of Singapore to inferior enemy forces. There must be no thought of sparing the troops or civil population and no mercy must be shown to weakness in any shape or form. Commanders and senior officers must lead their troops and, if necessary, die with them. There must be no question or thought of surrender. Every unit must fight it out to the end, and in close contact with the enemy. Please see that the above is brought to the notice of all senior officers and, by them, the troops. I look to you, and to your men, to fight to the end, to prove that the fighting spirit which won our Empire still exists to defend it.

signed: A. P. Wavell
General

Also on 10 February Lieutenant-General Tomoyuki Yamashita caused the following letter to be dropped by air:[1]

To the High Commander of the British Army in Malaya, Feb. 10th 2602

Your Excellency,

I, the Commander of the Nippon Army in Malaya, based on the spirit of Japan's chivalry, have the honour of presenting this note to your Excellency, advising you to surrender the whole forces in Malaya. My sincere respect is due to your army, which, true to the traditional spirit of Great Britain, is defending Singapore, which now stands isolated and unaided. Many fierce and fearless fights have been fought by your gallant men and officers, to the honour and glory of British warriorship. But the development of the general war situation has sealed the fate of Singapore and the continuation of futile resistance would only serve to inflict direct harm and injuries to thousands of non-combatants living in the city, and would certainly not add anything to the honour of your army. I expect that your Excellency will accept my advice, will give up this meaningless and desperate resistance and promptly order the entire front to cease hostilities, and will despatch at the same time your parliamentaire, according to the procedure shown at the end of this note. If, on the contrary, your Excellency should reject my advice, and the present resistance be continued, I shall be advised, though reluctantly from humanitarian consideration, to order my army to make annihilating attacks on Singapore. In closing this note, I pay my respects to your Excellency.

signed: Lt-Gen. Tomoyuki Yamashita
High Commander of the Nippon Army in Malaya

N.B. The Parliamentaire shall bear a large white flag and the Union Jack. The parliamentaire shall proceed along Bukit Timah Road.

The main water supply for Singapore Island came from the mainland in Johore and, since the Japanese were now in full control of the mainland, they simply had to close the valves to deprive the whole of the civilian population, as well as the army, of water, except for the little available from the MacRitchie Reservoir and one other small reservoir. The importance of this can be appreciated, as it was one of the chief reasons for what seemed to be an early surrender of all Allied forces. This is shown in General Percival's Order of the Day:

> It has been necessary to give up the struggle, and I want the reason explained to all ranks. The forward troops continue to hold their ground, but the essentials of war have run short. In a few days we shall have neither petrol nor food. Many types of ammunition have run short, and the water supply, on which the vast civilian population and many of the fighting troops are dependent, threatens to fail. This situation has been brought about, partly by being driven off our dumps and partly by hostile air attack and artillery action. Without these sinews of war we cannot carry on.
> I thank all ranks for their efforts during the campaign.
>
> *signed*: A. E. Percival, Lt-Gen.

There can be little doubt that the main reason for the capitulation must have been the shortage of petrol and the lack of water, coupled with the enemy's complete mastery in the air, as there proved to be vast supplies of ammunition which eventually fell into Japanese hands.

General Percival was known to be a brilliant tactician and, given the wherewithal, his name would probably have gone down gloriously in military history. However, with such limited resources available to him, he was incapable of holding Singapore and, at the surrender negotiations, he was a disillusioned and broken man. His last plea to General Yamashita was that he should guarantee the safety of the civilian population.

Cyril, now GSO2 to General Heath, played a major part in the events surrounding the final capitulation of Singapore. At the negotiations with the Japanese he was the only man present who could speak both languages fluently. Therefore, his hitherto unpublished report, written at the end of November 1945, demonstrates exactly what was said and what took place between 13 and 15 February 1942.

Cyril never kept a diary. There was no need to do so because he had a phenomenal memory and was thus able to write accurate accounts long after the events took place. His name will probably always be associated with the surrender at Singapore in February 1942 when, to his great sorrow, he carried the white flag of truce to Japanese headquarters at the Ford Motor Company factory at the foot of Bukit Timah hill.

NOTE ON THE CAPITULATION OF SINGAPORE
by Major C.H.D. Wild, Oxf. & Bucks Lt Infty.
(GSO 2 III Indian Corps)

1.   At about 21.00 hrs on 13 February 1942 Lt-Gen. Sir Lewis Heath, Comdg III Indians Corps, informed me that at a conference which he had had that day with Lt-Gen. A.E. Percival, GOC Malaya, it had become clear that if the situation continued to deteriorate we should have to ask for terms. He added that, as Malaya Command had sent all their Japanese-speaking officers out of the country, Gen. Percival had asked him if he had any such officer available, and that he had given my name. He then said: 'In case the situation arises, you must therefore hold yourself in readiness to go through the lines and make the first contact with the enemy, to arrange a meeting between their commander and Gen. Percival.'

2.   Late on the afternoon of 14 February 1942 the Corps Commander told me that he had heard that Malaya Command's interpreters had been evacuated because they had expressed the opinion that they would be in danger, if captured by the Japanese, because they had previously been resident in Japan. He most generously offered to evacuate me too if I shared their opinion. I did *not* share it; in fact I held the opposite view, that if there were any trouble from the Japanese after the capitulation, an officer who could speak their language would have a better chance of surviving it than anyone who could not. The Corps Commander, however, considered that the case of Lieut M. Ringer, IO Interpreter of III Indian Corps, was exceptional as he had been given a suspended sentence in Japan of six months imprisonment for alleged espionage. This officer was, therefore, evacuated that night. During the three and a half years of my captivity, although I was in daily and often acrimonious contact with the Japanese, I never heard more than half-jocular references to my supposedly clandestine activities in Japan before the war.

3.   Between 09.00 and 09.30 hrs on 15 February 1942 I accompanied the Corps Commander in my capacity as his GSO 2 (O) to the final conference in the underground 'battle-box' at Fort Canning. Lt-Gen.

A.E. Percival invited a review of the situation from the senior officers present. I recall in particular that Brigadier Simson (Chief Engineer) said that no more water would be available in Singapore from some time during the next day (16 February): also that the CRA said that Bofors ammunition would be exhausted by that afternoon (15 February), and that another class of ammunition, either 18 pdr or 25 pdr, was likewise practically exhausted. The decision to ask for terms was taken without a dissentient voice. Some minutes later, when details of the surrender were being discussed, Major-General Gordon Bennett, GOC 8th Australian Division, remarked: 'How about a combined counter-attack to recapture Bukit Timah?' This remark came so late, and was by then so irrelevant, that I formed the impression at the time that it was made not as a serious contribution to the discussion but as something to quote afterwards. It was received in silence and the discussion proceeded.

4. In particular, the time at which we should arrange to end hostilities was debated. When 16.00 hrs was suggested, General Heath objected that this was far too early, as the first party of parliamentaires had to make their way through the lines, contact Japanese GHQ and then return, having merely arranged for a subsequent meeting between Gen. Percival and the Japanese Commander. He suggested 20.00 hrs, but was overruled by Gen. Percival who approved of 16.00 hrs as the proposed time.

5. At the conclusion of the conference the Corps Commander turned me over to Malaya Command. I then accompanied Brigadier Newbigging from the 'battle-box'. We were joined by Mr Hugh Fraser, the Colonial Secretary, and with him, at about 11.30 hrs, entered an open roadster, containing a furled Union Jack and white flag, in which we were driven northwards up the Bukit Timah road until we were stopped by a mined road-block of Dannert wire across both the Bukit Timah and Dunnearn roads at the Adam road crossing. This formed the front line. From there we walked forward with the flags unfurled for about 600 yards up the Bukit Timah road until we were stopped by a Japanese patrol, who removed our pistols. I explained our mission and we were taken to a small villa about 100 yards west of the road, where a delay of an hour or more occurred while I insisted to various Japanese junior officers that we would deal with no-one except their GHQ, to which we demanded to be taken. Finally, Lt-Col Sugita of the Jap General Staff arrived with another officer, and Brigadier Newbigging handed over a letter from Lt-Gen. Percival.

6. Lt-Col Sugita then handed us a type-written letter with a one-page appendix. The letter requested Lt-Gen. Percival to meet Lt-Gen. Yamashita at Bukit Timah at... (the time was left blank). Brig. Newbigging inserted 16.00 hrs. The letter further stated that prior to this meeting the British Forces must comply with the orders given on the annexure. Towards the end of the discussion I drew Brig. Newbigging's attention to a clause in the annexure which stated that our forces must lay down their arms and remain in their positions. I pointed out that there was no reciprocal undertaking by the Japanese that they also would cease fire and stand fast. Brig. Newbigging permitted me to raise this point with Lt-Col Sugita, I did so and the following conversation took place in Japanese:

Sugita: (somewhat taken aback) 'There is no such undertaking by us in this document.'

Wild: 'That is why we are raising this point. Will you give us such an undertaking?'

Sugita: 'No. The document does not say so.'

Wild: 'How can Lt-Gen. Percival order his forces to lay down their arms, if the Japanese Army does not agree not to continue its advance against our unarmed troops?'

Sugita: 'You are not the negotiator!'

I reported my failure to Brig. Newbigging, who said: 'Leave it. It's getting late, and we must get back.'

7. During this discussion we received three shells in quick succession close to the villa from one of our own batteries. I learnt afterwards that a request to withhold shell-fire on the Bukit Timah road, made by Brig. Newbigging to the CRA as we left the 'battle-box', had narrowly averted a shoot by three regiments of artillery (72 guns) under Lt-Col S.W. Harris, RA, from the Adam road crossing northwards, at the time that we walked along this stretch (his counter-order reached his last battery two minutes before it was due to open fire).

8. Lt-Col Sugita then handed over a very large Japanese flag, with the order that it should be displayed from the top of the Cathay building as a signal to the Japanese that Gen. Percival had accepted the conditions and was on his way to meet the Japanese Commander. Sugita said that this would enable them to cease fire along the Bukit Timah road. I was

personally interested in this order as the Cathay building happened to house my Corps Headquarters. I therefore said: 'We cannot display it for more than ten minutes.' He replied: 'On the contrary, you must leave it there permanently.' I said: 'If we do our troops in the city will not know why it is there. They will shoot at it, or tear it down, and you will be angry afterwards.' He then said: 'Very well. Take it down after ten minutes.'

9. Finally Lt-Col Sugita asked if we had anything more to say. I replied: 'Only that we should have our weapons returned to us.' He bowed and we were given back our pistols. We were then blindfolded and driven back in a car to a point near the front-line. We again crossed the obstacles on foot and rejoined our car.

10. The return journey was uneventful, except for an inaccurate burst of pistol-fire, delivered at somewhat unsporting range, from a Provost Corporal of 18th Division, who opined that we were spies.

11. On reaching Fort Canning I was following Brig. Newbigging into Gen. Percival's room when I was intercepted by a Lt-Col (S & T) of Malaya Command, with whom I had had the most casual acquaintance when he was an RASC subaltern in my transport coming to Malaya sixteen months before. For some reason he chose this moment to make a most impertinent and ill-informed observation at the expense of the formation with which I had the honour to be serving. The minute or two which it took me to deal suitably with this interruption slightly delayed my entry into Gen. Percival's room, where I found Brig. Newbigging reporting on our expedition. The windows of this room looked out in the direction from which the enemy's batteries were firing. Some of their shells were bursting on the glacis of the fort below. I particularly admired the cool way in which Gen. Percival continued to sit at his desk when the concussion from a stick of bombs brought down some of the ceiling-boards and raised a cloud of dust in the room.

12. Brig. Newbigging turned to me and said: 'You had better get over to the Cathay to see about that flag. Get back as soon as you can as you will have to go out again with Gen. Percival.' I said: 'I shall be seeing my Corps Commander over there, so may I have the final orders regarding the time of ceasing fire?' He replied shortly: 'Orders on that point have already been sent out,' and resumed his conversation with the G O C. Attaching as I did so much importance to this question, I assumed that it had been the first point which he had raised with Gen. Percival, and that orders which I should learn on reaching Corps HQ had been issued

before I entered the room. It was already past 15.30 hrs. I drove across to the Cathay building by car. There was a certain amount of Japanese shell-fire on the way. When I reached the entrance to the Cathay I found that the vehicles in the car park had been burnt out: also the face of the building had been considerably scarred by shell-fire in my absence.

13. I reported to the Corps Commander the events of my recent mission. I had to tell him that I had been ordered to display the Japanese flag from the top of the building. I then asked what orders Malaya Command had sent regarding a postponement of the time of cease-fire. He replied that he had had none, but told me to find out from the Operations Room if any order had recently come in. I then walked up to the roof of the building. Some of the stairs were partially blocked with fallen masonry. On the roof I had the flag hung from the parapet on the side facing Bukit Timah and gave orders that it was not to be left there longer than the ten minutes stipulated. I then went down to the Operations Room, where I asked Major A.O. Robinson, the GSO 2(AD) who was the senior officer on duty there, what orders had been received regarding the cease-fire. He told me that no order had been received regarding the postponement of the time from 16.00 hrs, but I gathered from him that there was some doubt as to whether this was now to be the final time or not, and that he was unable to clarify the matter as the telephone line to Malaya Command was out of order. I said that as I was now going back to Malaya Command I would see that definite orders were sent to III Corps HQ before I left for Bukit Timah.

14. I got back to Fort Canning shortly after 16.00 hrs. Gen. Percival was seated at his desk and Brig. Torrance, the BGS, and Brig. Newbigging were standing beside it. They had been awaiting my return. I at once told Brig. Newbigging, in the hearing of the others, that III Corps were still without definite orders regarding the time of cease-fire and I asked that such orders should be sent to them. I received no reply whatever. No one else was speaking, and it appeared to me that Brig. Newbigging had chosen to ignore my question. As a last resort I appealed direct to Gen. Percival, who had got up and was standing behind his desk with his head bent forward. I said: 'If I may express an opinion myself, it is that we should not cease fighting until after you have seen the Japanese Commander at Bukit Timah.' I believe I added, and I know I thought, that even if the Japanese were annoyed when we met them at our not having ceased fire, this would be nothing in comparison with the risk of total disaster which we ran if our men disarmed themselves before

the terms of truce or capitulation were decided. Again my remarks were received in total silence. This was only broken when Gen. Percival (I think it was) said: 'We ought to go', and he and the two Brigadiers walked out of the room and down to the two cars which were awaiting us. I had no choice but to follow then.

15. Astonishing though this may sound, it was not altogether so to me, as I had become inured during the past week to seeing Gen. Percival's painful inability to give a decision, and on three occasions to make any reply whatever, when points of operational importance were referred to him, particularly by my Corps Commander.

16. As we drove up the Bukit Timah road I looked with interest to see whether the fighting was still in progress, as by then it was long after 16.00 hrs. I felt then and consider now that no-one in the two cars had the least idea whether the war was supposed to be over or not. There was some A A fire at low flying enemy aircraft and a little small arms fire: but I do not recall that there was any gunfire. Near the road everything was quiet. Some British Infantry of 18th Div. were coming down the road, carrying their weapons. Long after, their Company Commander told me that he had been warned that the cease-fire would be at 16.00 hrs, and he had regarded the sight of the first party going and returning past his position with a flag of truce as confirmation of this. As his troops were being mortared in their positions after 16.00 hrs he had elected to close on battalion headquarters without orders.

17. Again our party had to leave the cars and walk up the road until met by the Japanese. By that time it was so late that the Japanese had sent back the cars which they had brought to meet us, thinking that (as they said) Gen. Percival was not coming.

18. At the ensuing conference with Gen. Yamashita the second point raised by him was the question of when Gen. Percival would be prepared to cease hostilities. Gen. Percival said 22.00 hrs (23.30 hrs Tokyo time), while Yamashita wanted 20.30 hrs (22.00 Tokyo time). Gen. Percival gave way when he was told that he and Sir Shenton Thomas would have to come out as hostages if he insisted on the later hour. General Yamashita then openly expressed his relief that the earlier hour of 22.00 hrs (Tokyo time) had been accepted. He said: 'I can now tell you frankly that my assault on Singapore was timed to begin at midnight (Tokyo time) tonight. If you had declined to cease fighting until 23.30 hrs (Tokyo time) I should only have had thirty minutes in which to stop the advance and

might not have been able to halt it everywhere. As it is, I shall have time to order my forces to stand fast.'

19. After Gen. Percival and Brig. Torrance had returned to Singapore, I remained for some time at Bukit Timah with Brig. Newbigging. An opportunity occurred to take a quick look at a Japanese Staff-Officer's map of Singapore Island. From the blue pencil marks on this it appeared that the spear-head of the attack was to have thrust east of the Bukit Timah road, across the Golf Course and Mount Pleasant. Our 18th Division, defending this sector, had a total front of about 17,000 yds. Many of the troops were shaken. The Japanese had a considerable number of medium tanks available and six inch guns.

20. Alone of the four who took part in this capitulation I was privileged to be a witness of Gen. Itagaki's surrender to Admiral Lord Louis Mountbatten at Singapore in September 1945. Also, in the course of my work on war crimes, I had the pleasure of interrogating Gen. Yamashita in private at Manila in October 1945, on the day before his trial. He told me that he had three divisions on the island for this attack – on his left the Konoye Division (Lt-Gen. Nishimura); in the centre the 5th Division (Lt-Gen. Matsui); and on his right the 18th Division (Lt-Gen. Mutaguchi).

21. In all these circumstances few acquainted with the situation can doubt that had the attack gone in that night it would have broken clean through to the sea, splitting the garrison in two. The half-million citizens of Singapore would then have shared the fate of those of Nanking and Hangchow. As it was, Yamashita never allowed these three Divisions to enter the city after the capitulation.

22. The next morning (16 February) Gen. Heath came to me in Fort Canning and said: 'I want you to repeat carefully and clearly exactly what you said to me yesterday afternoon in the Cathay' (see para. 13). I did so. He said: 'That is exactly as I remember it', and then added that he had been severely taken to task by Gen. Percival that morning for the arrangements which he had made, due to his understanding that the cease-fire was to be at 16.00 hrs. I can only say that the astonishment with which I heard of this has persisted until today.

23. *Summary* (a) At the conference in the 'battle-box' on the morning of 15 February 1942, 16.00 hrs was the time selected by Gen. Percival for the cease-fire, in spite of Gen. Heath's objections (para. 4).

(b) No counter-order was received by III Indian Corps until 17.00 hrs; by which time, in the absence of any reply following my return to Fort Canning (para. 13), III Indian Corps had acted on that previous order and instructed 18th Div. and 11th Indian Div. to cease-fire. At 17.00 hrs a staff-officer came to Gen. Heath from Fort Canning and said that Gen. Percival had *not* ordered the cease-fire. Gen. Heath then countermanded his order to the two divisions.

(c) If this staff-officer was correct, why did Gen. Percival not tell me this when I, as a staff-officer of III Indian Corps, who had come straight from an interview with my commander, proposed precisely this postponement from 16.00 hrs (para. 14)? I do not believe that any Grade II staff-officer, particularly of a subordinate formation, could have pressed this matter harder than I did, especially as I repeated my request directly to the GOC Malaya, over the head and in the presence of a Brigadier who had just ignored it.

(d) From the moment of my argument with Lt-Col Sugita I was obsessed with the thought of my responsibility to my Corps Commander and to the troops of 18th Div. and 11th Indian Div. of ensuring that they were not over-run by a treacherous Japanese attack as a result of their having prematurely disarmed themselves. This anxiety did not diminish until I heard Gen. Yamashita, oblivious of the instructions contained in the letter which we had received from Sugita, ask the time at which Gen. Percival would be ready to cease-fire (para. 18). This certainly bore out my contention that the better course was to ignore Lt-Col Sugita's instructions.

24. *NOTE* Where in this narrative I have used inverted commas, I have recorded as nearly as possible the actual words which the speakers used. Elsewhere too this is a true and accurate account of the events of this unhappy day, so far as I was in a position to observe them.

NEW DELHI 30 November 1945

2/Lt Hishikari, a general's son, was Yamashita's official interpreter, but at these surrender negotiations his translations were very hesitant. Yamashita finally lost patience with him, banged his fist on the table and told Sugita to take over. There is a well-known photograph of Yamashita banging his fist on the table, apparently bullying Percival. In fact, Yamashita said that it was Hishikari's time-wasting hesitancy which infuriated him and he had no intention of bullying Percival. He was, of course, a very worried man as he was running out of ammunition. Delay could have shown up this deficiency and possibly revitalised the defence.

The defeat at Singapore cost the Allies the loss of nearly 140,000 British, Australian and Indian troops killed, wounded or captured, compared with 9,824 Japanese casualties. It must be remembered, however, that the Allies were exhausted by two months' continuous fighting and withdrawal, whereas the Japanese brought in wave upon wave of fresh soldiers.

To many the defence of Malaya and Singapore may appear to have lacked courage and a true fighting spirit on the part of the Allied troops, but modern warfare, such as it was at that time, could not be waged without air support. No-one can say that the Royal Navy could have fought their ships more courageously, but both the *Prince of Wales* and *Repulse* were a lost cause without air cover.

As it was known by the Prime Minister that Singapore could not be held, it seems strange that the two brigades of 18th Division, the 54th and 55th, reembarked in India to land in Singapore just before the capitulation. Was it to bring up the numbers of British prisoners-of-war to be more in line with those from the Commonwealth?

Upwards of 50,000 British and Australian troops alone became prisoners-of-war, and all the remaining European civilians who had not already been evacuated, approximately 3,500, were interned in Changi Gaol. 15 February 1942 was a black day indeed.

In my own case it was not until Christmas Eve, eleven months later, that my wife received official confirmation that I was a prisoner-of-war, and I am sure that this was so for most Allied servicemen. However, Celia and the Wild family learned of Cyril's fate very much earlier. David, a prisoner-of-war in Poland, saw a photo of Cyril carrying the white surrender flag in a German newspaper, and was able to write home with the news.

NOTE

[1] Lt-Col Ichiji Sugita drafted this letter for General Yamashita. He was not only a good linguist but also a brilliant soldier, and was Yamashita's Intelligence Officer on HQ 25th Army. Later, in 1961, he became Chief of Staff as a major-general in the Japanese Ground Self Defence Force.

Chapter 4
PRISONER-OF-WAR

What shall I think when I am called to die?
 Shall I not find too soon my life has ended?
The years, too quickly, have hastened by
 With so little done of all that I'd intended.
There were so many things I'd meant to try,
 So many contests I had hoped to win;
And, lo, the end approaches just as I
 Was thinking of preparing to begin.

Written by an unknown English youth in Singapore

The Japanese military had, for many years, been instilled with the notion that theirs was the superior race. Their warriors' ethic of *bushidō* was that they should never, under any circumstances, surrender, the only honourable alternative being suicide. It was a privilege to die gloriously in battle for their Emperor and their country, explaining why Kamikaze pilots went proudly to their deaths, but it was an everlasting disgrace to be taken prisoner. Thus, when the Allies surrendered the Japanese were amazed to find they suddenly had thousands of prisoners-of-war on their hands. In their eyes these men were beneath contempt, totally expendable, and would be used for their own ends regardless of the cost in human lives because the lives of such dishonourable men were of no consequence. The code of the Geneva Convention did not apply to the Japanese – they were the superior race.

Allied servicemen of the West were, therefore, totally unprepared for the brutal and heartless treatment they were about to receive from their captors of the East. Lack of understanding of an alien culture resulted in a legacy of bitterness that exists in many quarters to this day. Cyril, having lived in Japan for nine years, was certainly better prepared for what was to come, but surely even he could not have envisaged the degree of human cruelty to which the Japanese were prepared to sink, without shame.

Cyril claimed that the first two and a half years of his captivity were 'the best', as he was hard-worked all the time. This period included eight months on the Burma-Siam railway. He was kept in Fort Canning for a week after the capitulation in order to run messages between the Japanese and General Percival in Changi, to which camp he went daily. He received orders from General Yamashita through his staff officer, Colonel Sugita, with whom he had first crossed swords at the surrender negotiations. For this job he was given a car, with a pass and a liaison officer's armband, which allowed him to travel freely in Singapore, thus gaining a very good view of the Japanese occupation of the city.

Much of what he saw during those first few days was to prove invaluable as evidence in the major War Crimes Tribunal in Tokyo after the war. In his examination there by the counsel for the defence he was asked whether he had been obliged to sign any agreement not to escape, in return for his freedom of movement, and whether he had been accorded any special privileges. Cyril replied that, for precisely that reason, on one of his visits to Changi he had asked permission of his Corps Commander, General Heath, to make an escape. He certainly would have made an attempt, but was expressly ordered not to do so because of his exceptional ability as an interpreter and intelligence officer. He was proud of the fact that in all his three and a half years as a prisoner-of-war he never received preferential treatment. While at Fort Canning he shared a small clerk's office on the top floor with five British drivers and one other British officer, foraging for his own food and bedding.

50,000 British and Australian prisoners-of-war were concentrated in Changi, the Indian troops being segregated in a separate area, Nee Soon, probably with the intention of forcing them to join the 'Indian National Army'. Orders were issued that all POWs, irrespective of rank, were to salute Japanese and, later, Indian (INA) guards when they took over and, if not wearing caps and therefore unable to salute, they were made to bow low. British and Allied officers in Changi and other camps in Singapore were forbidden to wear badges of rank from February 1942 until April 1944.

On 20 February 1942 Cyril was ordered by Sugita to leave Fort Canning and move to the main POW encampment at Changi, where he lived with his Corps Commander and other staff officers in the old gunners' mess. He was attached to Malaya Command as Liaison Officer and Senior Interpreter. During this time at Changi Eric Lomax (9th Indian Division, Signals), who subsequently survived beatings and torture for operating a secret radio at Kanchanaburi on the Burma-Siam railway, was sent for by Cyril on his return from a working-party at Kranji, where POWs were building the Japanese war memorial. Cyril wanted to know all about their working conditions and anything of interest that Eric might have seen. It was the only time that Eric met Cyril and he remembers the occasion clearly. 'He was very much the intelligence officer, gathering up and storing information in his head for future reference.'

In March General Percival himself was taken away and shut up in a cell in Changi Gaol for four days, with no food, as he had refused to obey an order from General Yamashita's headquarters that he should provide British gunners to teach the Japanese how to use the Allied weapons that had fallen into their hands. At about this same time Lady Shenton Thomas, wife of the Governor General, was also being given particularly bad treatment, living in a small atap hut and dressed only in an old blouse, a skirt made of sacking and no footwear.

The men were becoming furious at the way Allied general officers were being treated, as General Heath too had been taken into Changi Gaol for interrogation. Cyril later testified:

> He told me that he had been interrogated by the Japanese at Changi Prison. He showed me a very dignified letter which he had written to the Japanese, explaining that he was unable to answer certain questions regarding the defences of India. He was then placed in a car and driven to Fort Canning where he was again interrogated by a Japanese major (Major Hayashi).
>
> In the course of this interrogation, when General Heath was not looking, the major came around the table and hit him a full-armed blow with his fist under the jaw. On the orders of the Japanese major he was then seized by four soldiers with rifles and bayonets who took him to an underground room in the precincts of Fort Canning. This was a small room which would normally have been air-conditioned, but at that time was without any ventilation whatever. An inch or so of water lay on the floor with, inevitably, a lot of mosquitoes. In this bare room a basin was fixed in the wall. The Japanese major came in, tested the water, and then went outside the cell and deliberately turned off the supply, thus depriving him of any means of washing or drinking. Lieutenant-General Sir Lewis Heath was then left there in the dark for 48 hours without food or water. At the time he was 56 or 57 and suffering from dysentery.

On 13 March Cyril marched twelve miles from Changi into Singapore to River Valley Road Camp, on a written order received from the Japanese by Malaya Command, nominating Cyril as the interpreter to accompany 1,500 men. River Valley Road was the first permanent working camp on Singapore Island, and Cyril remained there for eight months serving, under the command of Lieutenant-Colonel C.P. Heath, as Brigade Major, Interpreter and Liaison Officer of the combined camps of

River Valley Road and Havelock Road. (Colonel Heath should not be confused with General Sir Lewis Heath, who had been Cyril's Corps Commander.) The camp was on reclaimed marsh land within the limits of the city, and the huts which accommodated them had been built before the war.

These huts were roofed with atap and the walls, made of palm leaves, were eaten away by ants in a very short time. Wooden planking running down two sides of an earthen gangway formed the platforms on which the men slept side by side, about 2' 6" being the maximum space available per man. Upwards of 200 men occupied each hut, which were 120 feet long, with no bedding or sleeping mats provided. Owing to a plague of bedbugs the men chose to sleep outside in fine weather.

Initially there was no sanitation whatsoever and the sudden tropical storms made the whole area water-logged. In these dreadful conditions the prisoners were told to make their own latrines by scratching holes in the ground with their hands, and this lack of hygiene resulted in an early outbreak of dysentery. Cyril had been promised personally by the Japanese before leaving Changi that tools would be supplied to them and that it would be unnecessary to take any with them. The Ikari *butai* did indeed have an enormous store of spades, picks, changkuls, etc. within 50 yards of the camp, but it was a week before Cyril could persuade Lieutenant Fukada to let the men use them. After two weeks Cyril was able to get the place drained and, in the meantime, the municipality supplied several hundred lidded buckets. By April 1942 the numbers were up to 4,500 in a space 130 yards by 180 yards, and the peak number in that camp became 6,000.

Havelock Road Camp was similar, with 3,500 men, and was joined to River Valley Road by a wooden bridge and a road, covering about a quarter of a mile, both of which were built by the prisoners. The bridge crossed the Singapore River which, at this point, was a narrow stream. Both camps became, in effect, one camp and the POW headquarters was a small purpose-built hut on the River Valley Road side of the bridge.

The main work for the prisoners, from March to December 1942, was in the docks, loading and unloading ships. The supplies coming in included ammunition, and looted material was being shipped back to Japan.

On 29 July an incident occurred. All men in Havelock Road, including a number whom the Japanese had agreed need not go out to work as they had no boots, also sick men and the chaplain, were marched to a field just outside River Valley Road camp, whither Colonel Heath and Cyril were summoned. They were taken to a newly formed car park, surfaced with broken brick and a certain amount of broken glass, and were made to run round in a circle. Cyril managed to persuade the Japanese officer to detach the medical orderlies, cooks and some of the sick and finally to stop it altogether. The Japanese officer then said: 'I have taught you to dance in bare feet. Now you will work in bare feet.'

Until September 1942 the prisoners were under the control of 25th Army HQ, but were then told that they had become 'real prisoners-of-war', taken over by an administration centred on Tokyo, under the command of Major-General Fukuye. That month all POWs in River Valley Road and Havelock Road camps were ordered to sign a form promising not to attempt to escape. Knowing that this was completely illegal, Colonel Heath and Cyril asked for permission to go to Changi to consult with Lieutenant-Colonel E.B. Holmes (Manchester Regiment), who was the senior British and Allied commander in the camp. (In August 1942 the IJA had issued an order that all senior officers above the rank of Lieutenant-Colonel would be transferred to Formosa.) This they were allowed to do and Colonel Holmes, having explained to them what had just happened the previous week at Selerang, advised Colonel Heath not to let his men suffer the same treatment that they had undergone, and to allow them to sign under duress.

What has now become widely known as the 'Selerang Incident' was a truly barbaric act perpetrated by Major-General Fukuye, who was determined, at any cost, to force all Allied prisoners-of-war to sign a form or, as the Japanese termed it, a 'parole', promising not to escape under any circumstances. Having recently taken over command of Malayan POW camps he must have lost face when two Australian and two British servicemen attempted to escape from Bukit Timah camp. After rowing for several days in a small boat they had been recaptured, but were allowed back into camp to live as any other prisoners-of-war. However, Fukuye decided to use these men to his own advantage in his determination to prevent further escapes and to ease the Japanese conscience when using the ultimate deterrent.

On 2 September he issued orders that all POWs, except about 1,000 hospital cases and certain doctors and medical orderlies, should immediately move to Selerang Barracks. Lieutenant-Colonel S.W. Harris, OBE, in a sworn statement used by the prosecution in the subsequent trial of Lieutenant-General Fukuye, stated:

On 2 September 1942 I was commanding 18th Divisional Area of Changi POW Camp under Colonel Holmes as Commander of this camp. In the morning we were engaged in preparations for the move to Selerang, which was to be completed that day, as a result of refusal to sign the undertaking not to attempt escape. Colonel Holmes and his area commanders were ordered to attend the execution of the four men, Corporal Breavington, AIF, Private Gale, AIF, Private Walters, East Surrey Regt, and Private Fletcher, RAOC, and I attended as Commander of 18th Division Area. The site was on the seashore near the Beting Kusha anti-aircraft practice-ground. In the party was Holmes, myself, Lt-Col Galleghan, commanding AIF, Lt-Col Tawney and Lt-Col Jephson. The time was about midday. Three men arrived simultaneously with us in a car. Also present a Japanese colonel, Lt Okasaki, a Japanese interpreter and other Japanese officers. These stood apart from us, laughing, joking and smoking cigarettes. After half an hour the fourth to be executed arrived, dressed in pyjamas jacket. One of the four was too weak to stand and had to be supported by two of his comrades. Breavington addressed the Japanese officers, and while he was doing so a party of three Indians and an Indian officer arrived. Breavington said: "These men are not guilty. I was responsible for the whole escape. Shoot me and let them go." No reply was made...

The execution took place in the most barbaric manner, the Sikh firing squad being extremely inefficient and inaccurate. The men were not blindfolded and were wounded in the arms and stomach before finally being killed. They had never been tried by court martial. When it was all over the Allied officers were addressed by Lt Okasaki. He said words to the effect that they had seen what happened and that it was their duty to order their men to sign the required promise of non-escape. The officers were then allowed back to Changi to continue with preparations for the move to Selerang.

Between fifteen and sixteen thousand prisoners were concentrated into an area designed to accommodate under 900 men, a barracks which had previously housed one battalion of the Gordons. There were no latrines or washing facilities, and a fire hydrant a few yards off the square was forbidden to the prisoners. Work was immediately started to dig latrines in the tarmacadam square, and space was so limited that men had to live and sleep within a few yards of this area, but still they were not broken and refused to sign.

General Fukuye's next move was to announce that all sick from the hospital, including infectious cases, should be sent to Selerang. At that particular period diphtheria was of epidemic proportions. Food rations were drastically reduced. After four days Colonel Holmes, on the advice of medical officers, ordered everyone to sign the 'parole' under duress because, by that time, men were dying from disease and having to be buried within the narrow confines of the barrack square.

After the war Lieutenant-General Fukuye was found guilty at his trial, at which Cyril himself gave evidence, and was sentenced to death. On 27 April 1946 he was taken to the same spot where he had ordered the execution of the four men. Fukuye died instantly, after shouting the obligatory '*Banzai!*' (Ten Thousand Years!), which referred to the longevity of the Japanese Emperors. Ten Australian servicemen witnessed the death of perhaps the only war criminal to be shot rather than hanged.

Cyril wrote later:

> Altogether, 15,000 POWs passed through the camps (River Valley and Havelock Road) in eight months, 9,000 British, 5,000 Australians and 1,000 Dutch. I went back to Changi with 5,000 for four months in December 1942, where I found the rump of Malaya Command still referring to themselves by all their old titles, AAG, DDST, etc. and having no contact with the Japs except by letters, of which they were despatching upwards of ten a day, and never getting an answer! In face of great difficulties from my own side (and none from the Japs!) I reestablished direct liaison, and by April 1943 things were going so well – and life in consequence was so dull – that I volunteered to go with F Force to Thailand.

Cyril had already heard something of the hardships and deprivation suffered by those building the railway from men sent to Outram Road Gaol from Siam and evacuated back to Changi for illness, but:

> For me it was a job worth doing and an adventure in its way. Certainly there was never a moment when I regretted being there: but 3,100 dead out of 7,000 in eight months was a heavy price to pay.

Brave words that conceal the degree of suffering endured by everyone on F Force. POWs have always tended to gloss over their treatment, feeling that nobody could appreciate the reality of the conditions unless they had been there themselves. This explains the strong bond that exists between all Far-East POW survivors today, their motto being: 'To keep going the spirit that kept us going.'

For their invasion of Burma in 1942 the Japanese used the one road that was possible for motor traffic in dry weather, and several jungle tracks. After occupying Burma they realised that in order to maintain their forces in that country and mount any further military operations there they required a better overland line of communication. They decided to build a chord-line, linking the Siam and Burma railway systems, the official title of which was the 'Thai-Burma Rail Link Line'.

On 20 June 1942 the Imperial Japanese Army GHQ in Tokyo indicated the essentials of its construction as:

(i) to ensure a land supply route to Burma and to develop a commercial transportation route to Burma and Thailand;

(ii) to extend 400 km. from Nong Pladuk in Thailand to Thanbyuzayat in Burma;

(iii) to carry a daily load of c. 3,000 tons;

(iv) to be completed by the end of 1943;

(v) to use construction materials available in the area with other necessary materials to be supplied by the Thai and Japanese governments: to cost 700m. yen.

Labour needed was laid down as local coolies and prisoners-of-war, as appropriate.

Plans for such a railway had been investigated early this century by British engineers. One ran from Burma to Pitsanlok in northern Thailand, another *via* the Three Pagodas Pass, the third being from Victoria Point. The Japanese plan followed the British second plan in principle. Local Thai were sceptical about its success, not least because of the climatic conditions, the region of Tenasserim being in the world's heaviest rain belt.

Now, however, the construction of the railway was regarded by the Japanese High Command as of great urgency, and Emperor Hirohito himself was said to have decreed that it was to be driven through in the minimum time, regardless of cost. They determined to build the railway without machinery, using the vast source of slave labour they had at their disposal. In the event they did it in one year; six months under the scheduled time, but at a cost the world will never forget.

It ran for 415 km. through mountainous jungle, rose to about 275 metres above sea level, and was built by manpower using picks, changkuls, shovels, gunpowder, cold chisels and mallets, saws, derricks and pulleys, with local cement-mixers for concrete well-crib bridge-piers. Rails came mainly from the Malayan eastern seaboard line, steel bridge-trusses from Java and Sumatra, sleepers were cut from local timber, ballast from river shingle-beds and broken rock cuttings.

Work on the construction of the railway began both from Burma in the north and Thailand in the south. Movement of prisoners-of-war to become labourers on the railway began on 14 May 1942 when A Force, 3,000 Australians under Brigadier A.L. Varley, AIF, embarked from Singapore harbour for Moulmein and were joined off Malacca Straits by the British Sumatra POW Battalion under Capt. Dudley P. Apthorp, R. Norfolks, who were an escape party from Singapore who got no further than Sumatra.

Between October 1942 and March 1943 more than 35,000 men of various nationalities either left Changi prison camp or passed through on their way north. Those destined for work in Burma went by sea to Moulmein and those for Siam by rail to Banpong. Smaller parties went by other routes. 61,106 British, Australian, American and Dutch POWs worked on the railway, together with many thousands of native coolies.

In the spring of 1943 the Allied navies were gaining control of the Indian Ocean, and thus the one supply line for the Japanese invasion of India became increasingly difficult to maintain. This made it imperative for them to expedite the completion of the railway, necessitating considerable reinforcements in the work force. The 'Speedo!' was on.

Early in 1943, therefore, the senior officers at Changi were told to produce 7,000 men to be moved to Siam. They replied that it would not be possible to find so many fit men for a working-party. However, the order issued by Major-General Arimura, successor to Major-General Fukuye as GOC Allied Prisoners-of-War in Malaya, ran thus:

(i) The reason for the move was that the food situation in Singapore was difficult, and that it would be far better in the new place.

(ii) This was not a working-party.

(iii) As there were not seven thousand fit combatants in Changi, 30% of the party were to be 'unfit' men, unfit to march or work. The unfit men would have a better chance of recovery with better food, and in a pleasant hilly country, with good facilities for recreation.

(iv) There would be no marching, except for short distances from train to nearby camp, and transport would be provided for baggage and men unfit to march.

(v) A military band was to be taken.

(vi) All tools and cooking gear, and an engine and gear for electric light were to be taken.

45

(vii) Gramophones, blankets, clothing and mosquito nets would be issued at the new camps.

(viii) A good canteen would be available in each camp after three weeks. Canteen supplies for the first three weeks were to be bought with prisoners' money before leaving Singapore.

(ix) The party would include a medical party of about 350, with equipment for a central hospital for 400 patients, and a medical supply for three months.

As a general rule, the fitter elements of the population of Changi had been sent on the earlier parties, but with the promise of better conditions and the fact that there were fewer men left in Changi, about 2,000 unfit men were included in F Force. However, the majority of the other 5,000 had also been ill since the capitulation, many of them being recent convalescents from such diseases as diphtheria, dysentery and beri-beri. All were reduced in strength by malnutrition during the previous year.

Thus, on 18 April 7,000 men of the ill-starred F Force, under Lt-Col S.W. Harris, RA, comprising 3,334 British (many from 18th Division) and 3,666 Australians, began to leave Singapore by train. The first train carrying H Force followed on 5 May, under Lt-Col H.R. Humphries, RA, 1,411 British, 670 Australians and 588 Dutch, with two further small medical parties of mixed nationalities, K and L Forces, leaving on 25 June and 24 August respectively.

Each day, for thirteen days, 600 F Force prisoners were crowded into steel rice trucks, which were totally enclosed apart from double sliding doors on one side. The 27 to 30 men in each box-car allowed little room for sitting, and certainly only a very few could lie down at the same time. There was no form of sanitation, and the many who were suffering from dysentery could only hang out of the sliding door as the train went along, which, fortunately, had a chain stretched across the opening on which to cling. Otherwise, there were occasional stops when everyone relieved themselves at the side of the track and, if feeling strong enough, attempted a few physical exercises to try and stimulate the circulation. The journey lasted four to five days.

Food consisting of rice and onion water was normally provided twice a day, but on the last leg of the journey no food or water was available for 24 hours. During the day the sun beat down on the sheet metal making an almost unbearable heat, but at night the cold was intense.

Cyril, as a member of F Force, wrote his own report, probably with the idea of using it in evidence at any future was crimes trial, and surely it must be the most accurate and concise of any that were written.

As each party arrived at Banpong it learnt that the Force was faced with a march of indefinite length, as no transport was available. Consequently all the heavy equipment of the Force, including hospital equipment, medical supplies, tools and cooking gear, and all personal kit which could not be carried on the man, had to be abandoned in an unguarded dump at Banpong. Practically the whole of this material (including three quarters of the medical stores) was lost to the Force throughout the eight months spent up-country, as the immediate advent of the monsoon (at the usual season) prevented the Japanese from moving more than a negligible proportion. of it by lorry.

The march of 300 kilometres which followed would have been arduous for fit troops in normal times. For this Force, burdened with its sick and short of food, it proved a trial of unparalleled severity. The road had a loose metal surface for the first two stages but then degenerated into an old elephant track, widened into a hazardous dry weather trail, through dense and mountainous jungle. The march was carried out in stages of 20 to 30 kilometres and lasted two and a half weeks. The parties always marched at night; the monsoon broke in earnest soon after the march began, and conditions rapidly worsened. Everyone was loaded to capacity and such medical equipment of the Force as could be carried was distributed to individuals. Men toiled through the pitch blackness and torrential rain, sometimes knee-deep in water, sometimes staggering off bridges in the dark; sprains and bruises were common, fractures of arms and legs occurred, and stragglers were set upon and looted by marauding Thais. Of the large and growing number of sick, many fell by the wayside, and they and their kit had to be carried by their comrades.

At the staging-camps, which were merely roadside clearings in the jungle, there was no overhead cover; it was sometimes a long carry for water, and it was impossible for men to rest properly. Food generally consisted of rice and onion stew, with hot water to drink, and often of rice only. This was insufficient to maintain health and entirely inadequate to support the physical strain of a march of this description. These staging-camps were in charge of truculent Japanese N C Os, who demanded large fatigue parties when the men should have been resting, and forcibly drove the sick on to the road with blows to continue the march night after night, in spite of the protests of their officers.

No arrangements existed at any camps for accepting those who were too ill to continue with the march. At Tarsao a Japanese medical lieutenant agreed that 30 men were incapable of proceeding further, and issued written orders to this effect to the I J A corporal in charge of the camp. The corporal refused to obey the order. Cyril and an Australian doctor, Major Bruce Hunt of Perth, made strenuous efforts on behalf of those desperately sick men, but were themselves severely beaten up by the corporal. A bone in Major Hunt's hand was broken. Their brave action produced little effect, but at least a few were allowed to remain at Tarsao.

Major Bruce Hunt's written statement says:

> At the time scheduled for parade I fell in the 37 severely ill men apart from the main parade. Major Wild and I stood in front of them. The corporal approached with a large bamboo in his hand and spoke menacingly to Major Wild, who answered him quietly. The corporal's reply was to hit Major Wild in the face. Another guard followed suit and, as major Wild staggered back, the corporal thrust at his genitalia with his bamboo. One guard tripped me while two others pushed me to the ground. The three then set about me with bamboos, causing extensive bruising of skull, back, hands and arms and a fractured 5th metacarpal bone.

Cyril, aware that Western logic was intellectual whereas Japanese logic was emotional, was never deterred by his own rough treatment and continually acted in what he thought was the best interest of others. The Japanese called him 'the tall man who never slept', an apt description of a man who worked ceaselessly to help his fellow men.

> On arrival at the destination, five jungle camps spread over a distance of 50 kilos in close proximity to the Thailand-Burma border, it was found that the camps had not been completed. All ranks were housed in unroofed huts, exposed to the continual downpour of the monsoon rains, which continued without intermission for the next five months. From most of these camps men were taken out to work by the Japanese engineers as soon as they arrived, without opportunity to rest, although many of them had just completed six successive night marches, and were in the last stages of exhaustion.
>
> Unlike all other POWs in Thailand, F Force remained nominally under the administration of Major-General Arimura's headquarters at Changi, Singapore.

Cyril always felt, and indeed said so later in his evidence at Tokyo, that by not transferring F Force to the administration of the Major-General commanding prisoners-of-war in Siam, both generals evaded the real responsibility for the disaster of that Force.

> The local Japanese commander was Lt-Col Banno, who proved incapable either of administering the Force or of protecting its personnel from the outrageous demands of and treatment by the Japanese engineers, under whom it was put to work. The camps were commanded by junior Japanese officers or N C Os of the Malayan Administration and the guards were Koreans. The former, with one exception,[1] were entirely subservient to the engineers, or themselves actively hostile, while some of

the Koreans also treated the prisoners with senseless cruelty. The officers and men of the engineers, whose sole responsibility to the prisoners was to make them work, behaved with calculated and extreme brutality from start to finish.[2]

Cholera broke out in the first camp early in May. This was directly attributable to the criminal negligence of the Japanese. For at Konkoita, the last staging camp but two, every one of the fifteen marching parties was forced to camp for one or more days within a few yards of huts filled with hundreds of cholera stricken coolies, on ground covered with infected faeces, where the air was black with flies. British officers asked for the loan of spades to remove this filth, but the Japanese replied contemptuously, "use your hands". Lt-Col Harris protested vigorously to Lt-Col Banno, warning him of the inevitable consequences, and demanding that either all forward movement should be stopped or that the infection point should be by-passed. But nothing was done; the march forward continued, and by the end of May cholera was epidemic in all five labour camps.

The work demanded of all men, without consideration of their physical condition, was heavy navvy-labour on the rushed construction of a 50 kilo stretch of the Burma-Thailand railway, through hilly and flooded jungle, immediately south of the Three Pagodas Pass. This work was arduous in the extreme, men having to carry logs far beyond their strength and pile-drive up to their waists in water. The hours were generally from first light to dark, but frequently men were kept out as late as 2.00 a.m. the following morning. Men working in quarries without boots had their feet badly cut and these cuts developed into tropical ulcers. Through incessant work in deep mud, trench feet became practically universal and rapidly developed into ulcers also.

There were daily beatings of officers and men at work, sometimes even into unconsciousness. These beatings were not for disciplinary purposes but were intended to urge sick and enfeebled men to physical efforts quite beyond their remaining strength, or to punish officers for intervening on their behalf.

Every morning the same grim spectacle was repeated in the various camps of parading men for work at first light. Emerging from their crowded huts or leaky shelters in the pouring rain, even the fitter men appeared gaunt and starving, clad in rags or merely loincloths, most of them bootless and with cut and swollen feet. In addition, some 50 or 60 sick men from "hospital", leaning on sticks or squatting in the mud, would be paraded to complete the quota, and would become the subject of a desperate argument between their officers and the Japanese engineers. Sometimes all of these, sometimes only a part, would be taken out to work and would leave the camp hobbling on sticks or half carried by their comrades.

Many of the fitter men had not seen their camp in daylight for many weeks, and had had no opportunity of washing themselves or their clothes.

Cyril was attached to F Force Headquarters at Nieke as an additional staff officer and senior interpreter, his role being to suggest methods of presenting problems to the Japanese. He was invaluable to POWs, because it was not only his mastery of the language but also his understanding of the curious thought-processes and violent emotionalism of the Japanese that often enabled him to save them from the brutal treatment meted out by guards and engineers, sometimes earning himself a beating for his selfless efforts. In the words of one man, 'he seemed to be able to tame the Japs and spent much of his time battling with them on behalf of the prisoners. From personal knowledge I know that he saved several men from having their hands chopped off.'

For the last four months of his time on the railway Cyril was up at Sonkurai Camp, he, Colonel Harris and Colonel Dillon having been despatched up there by Banno, who was extremely tired of being constantly bombarded with their protests and demands. In a letter dated October 1945 he wrote of Sonkurai:

> . . . the damage was already done: and we won our battle there too late, as 500 men were already dying in one hut when our little Force HQ – Lt-Cols Harris and Dillon and I – arrived there. In Thailand, as everywhere else, I was very lucky in being with first-rate chaps; and the troops, with whom I had more to do than most by virtue of my job, were really grand.

At a few of the camps, as in Changi, there were brave and dedicated men who risked their lives to operate secret radios, and the news they disseminated, as the Allied cause improved, was a tremendous morale booster for us all. At Kanchanaburi one such radio was discovered and eight men were arrested, in two groups on 29 and 31 August respectively. Captain Jack Hawley and Lt Armitage were beaten to death. Lt Eric Lomax had both arms broken. He and the other survivors of the party were subsequently court-martialled in Bangkok and taken to Outram Road Gaol, Singapore, to serve five years' sentences.

More fortunate was James Mudie of the BBC, who operated a radio at Sonkurai camp, keeping it hidden in the cholera isolation camp. The Japanese were terrified of this disease and kept well clear of the 'hospital' and isolation area. Mudie felt confident, perhaps too confident:

> I got a bit casual. During the day I usually hid the radio in a latrine, but one morning when the set, a battery, a coil of wire and a pair of pliers were in my hut, I heard a bugle call which was the arranged emergency warning that the Japs had started a search. Fortunately, a friend smuggled the radio out, but the Nips found the other things. I knew I was for it, so I quickly got word to Cyril Wild. He didn't attempt to explain. He simply told the Jap officers that the battery, wire and pliers were part of the hospital equipment and were used to set up lights for emergency night operations. They believed him and the hospital was even allowed to keep this 'equipment'.

THAILAND – BURMA RAILWAY

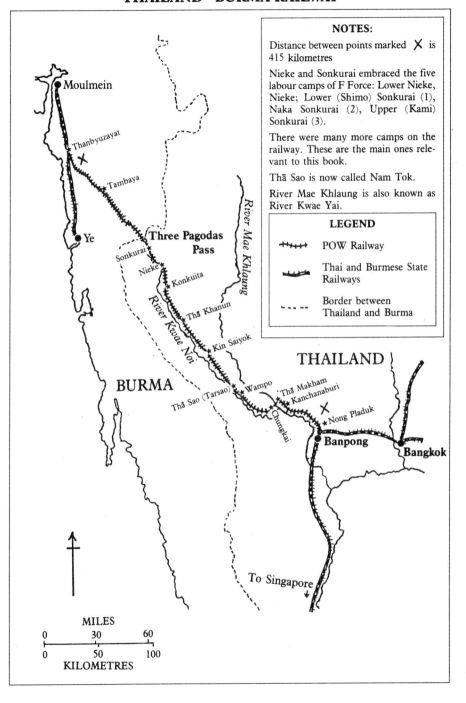

NOTES:

Distance between points marked ✕ is 415 kilometres

Nieke and Sonkurai embraced the five labour camps of F Force: Lower Nieke, Nieke; Lower (Shimo) Sonkurai (1), Naka Sonkurai (2), Upper (Kami) Sonkurai (3).

There were many more camps on the railway. These are the main ones relevant to this book.

Thā Sao is now called Nam Tok.

River Mae Khlaung is also known as River Kwae Yai.

LEGEND

++++ POW Railway

━━ Thai and Burmese State Railways

- - - - Border between Thailand and Burma

Moulmein

Thanbyuzayat

Tambaya

Ye

Three Pagodas Pass

River Mae Khlaung

Sonkurai

Nieke

Konkuita

Thā Khanun

River Kwae Noi

Kin Saiyok

BURMA

THAILAND

Thā Sao (Tarsao)

Wampo

Thā Makham

Kanchanaburi

Chungkai

Nong Pladuk

Banpong

Bangkok

To Singapore

MILES

0   30   60

0   50   100

KILOMETRES

Mudie described Cyril as a man of great integrity:

> He was extremely sensitive, had a great sense of humour, a commanding, challenging presence and, to put it simply, breeding. Even the Japanese officers respected him, particularly for those last two characteristics, as well as for his ability to talk their own language. He understood the Japanese officer class and could handle them – and they knew it.

For the working parties at Sonkurai, which was merely a jungle clearing on the banks of the Huai Ro Khi River, the day began at dawn with a trudge of anything up to eight miles through deep mud after the selection of men 'fit' to work on the line. A man with something to show, such as a blood-covered bandage round his leg, had a better chance of being excused work than a man dying of dysentery or malaria, although in some cases the Japanese engineers would kick the wound dressing to see if he screamed with pain, before excusing him work for the day. They would literally drive out, with sticks or weapons, men who were almost incapable of walking.

They were put to work on clearing jungle, cutting down trees, adzing timber, driving piles, loading elephants, carting earth and moving rocks. Levelling of the track involved carrying all materials by hand in flat baskets or on stretchers, tools being few and simple. The stretch of railway being constructed included the building of a three-span wooden trestle-bridge, held together with iron spikes driven in with heavy hammers. There were no nuts and bolts, and building methods were extremely primitive, but in spite of this all the bridges that were built withstood the weight of the trains.

At the short midday rest, sometimes of only a few minutes, they ate some cold boiled rice and a few beans. Then they worked till dark, driven on with blows from fists, rifle-butts, sticks and wire whips. Men were permanently shouted at, *Kora!* (Here you!), *Baka yaro!* (Fool!), forced to work at bayonet point in the intense heat and pouring rain until they literally dropped in their tracks. If a man died at work he had to be carried back to camp to be counted at roll-call, before being allowed to be cremated or buried. If thought to be slacking, men were made to stand holding heavy rocks above their heads and, if they dropped them, would be beaten.

After dark came the march back to camp, where wounds and sores were examined by firelight. Supper, usually at 10 p.m., but often much later, was again rice, beans and weak tea, occasionally supplemented with a minute quantity of 'yak'. At night the men slept, crowded together, on bamboo slats in huts full of bugs and lice.

The sanitation was indescribable. Latrine pits were over-flowing because of constant use and monsoon rains, and the approach to them from the huts was fouled by men whose dysentery was so intense that they just could not reach the latrines in time. The camp was a morass of black mud, seething with maggots. 'Living conditions' would be a misnomer – there were no living conditions.

The POW headquarters, under Lt-Col S. W. Harris, OBE, RA, was handicapped by the obstinacy of the Japanese in refusing access to the various camps, and by Lt-Col Banno's failure to make protests felt by the engineers or to ameliorate conditions himself as required. Written protests and appeals to Major-General Arimura were never answered. Only once was direct access to the regimental commander of the engineers obtained,[3] and that by chance, when a personal appeal by Lt-Col Harris and his staff resulted in the postponement of an order which would have caused the immediate and permanent expulsion of 700 desperately sick and dying men from their hospital hut into open jungle during the worst of the monsoon rains, to make way for a native labour force. This order had already been endorsed by Lt-Col Banno's administration.

The hospital, so-called, in every camp was nothing but a dilapidated hut with leaky roof, no walls or lighting, and with split bamboo staging on which the men were crammed, their bodies touching one another. In these grossly over-crowded conditions even such few mosquito nets as the Japanese provided could not be used, with the result that over 90% of the Force were speedily infected with malaria. Sleeping mats and blankets were never made available except in negligible quantities.

The attitude of the Japanese towards the sick was a mixture of callous indifference and active spite; for their sickness they were regarded as impeding the Japanese war effort. Two remarks made, at official interviews, by Lt Fukuda,[4] commander of one of the camps, will serve to illustrate this attitude: "International law and the Geneva Convention do not apply if they conflict with the interests of the Japanese army."; and again (to a senior Australian medical officer), "You have in the past spoken somewhat boastfully of the Geneva Convention and humanity. You must remember that you are our prisoners-of-war, that you are in our power, and that under present circumstances these things do not apply."

Although cholera killed approximately 750 of the Force, by far the most deadly disease was dysentery, aggravated by malnutrition, and generally complicated by malaria or beri-beri or both. Over a long period no food was available for such patients except rice and beans, and the quantities provided for the sick were deliberately reduced by the Japanese to starvation point, in the expressed belief that this would compel them to go out to work. The inevitable result was that hundreds of men died in a condition of extreme emaciation and complete despair.

By 20 June, two months after leaving Changi, only 700 men of the Force were out at work and most of these were sick, while the remainder, except for the small administrative and medical parties, were lying in improvised "hospitals" in each of the labour camps.

I too was a member of this ill-fated force and, in due course, was to know at first hand how Cyril Wild could handle the Japanese authorities.

In May 1943 I was one of the 1,600 British prisoners-of-war at Sonkurai Camp 2, the fourth of the five labour camps to which Cyril refers. After the cholera outbreak a Japanese medical party arrived and 'glass-rodded' us, a crude method of ascertaining which men were cholera carriers and, unfortunately, my test proved positive. Although shattered by this news, I wasn't surprised as I had most of the symptoms of cholera but had not died within 24 hours, which seemed to be the normal period of survival.

On the evening of 5 June we were ordered to move out of the camp immediately and to form an isolation camp on the opposite side of the railway trace, near the hospital hut, about five or six hundred yards away. The senior officers appealed that at least the sick and dying should be left where they were until the following morning, but this was refused. So the move took place, in torrential rain, and many died that night. Daylight next morning revealed that our new site had been the cremation area for the coolies and was littered with partly burned bodies.

We spent most of each day cutting wood to build pyres, and death came so quickly that men helping in the morning were themselves being cremated that same evening. As we could no longer work on the railway, the Japanese saw no reason why they should provide us with any rations. We were kept alive solely on rice that the active men deducted from their own food and, although the Japs knew that this was being brought over to us, they didn't stop it.

My commanding officer, Lt-Col M.T.L. Wilkinson, RE, often came across to see me after dark, despite the risks and penalties. He felt strongly that an escape should be attempted, in order to let the outside world know how prisoners were forced to work at tasks far beyond their human capacity, and the conditions under which they lived and died. Wilkie asked me if I would join him in such an attempt, if he could get together a party of about ten. It was not an easy decision. I knew my chances of survival were slim if I stayed, but I was determined, at any cost, to return to my wife and small son. I agreed.

The party included Capt. W.H. Anker, RASC, 18th Division, two others from his unit, Capt. J.H. Feathers and Lt J.F. Robinson, Lt I.M. Moffat, Queen Victoria's Own Madras Sappers and Miners, 9th Indian Division, Lt G. Machado, Straits Settlement Volunteer Force,

Lt T.P.D. Jones, Malay Regiment, Cpl Brown, SSVF, and an Indian fisherman, Nur Mahommed.

From a map on a silk handkerchief we estimated we were about 80 kilometres from Ye on the Burma coast, which we hoped to cover in three weeks. Bill Anker, in charge of the cookhouse, had been able to save food to be stored at my cholera isolation camp, safe from the Japanese. A prismatic compass, built into the false bottom of my water bottle, together with three parangs, formed our total equipment.

In my isolation camp, under cover of the noise of the men's axes cutting timber, I was able to cut a path into the jungle to give us a good start. I reached a small river, which we hoped would cover our tracks, before finding a place to reenter the jungle on the far bank. Each of us, individually, agreed that if we became a casualty we should have to be abandoned. A hard decision, but necessary if anyone was to succeed.

On 5 July 1943, just before dawn, Wilkie and the rest came across, one at a time. We were now committed, success or death. Each carried a pack with blanket, ground sheet and part of our rations. We had allowed four ounces of rice a day for three weeks, with a few tins of fish. Most of us also carried a small haversack with our personal items. We said no goodbyes, not wanting anyone else to be involved. We knew there would be repercussions, but felt this risk was justified if we could contact the free world.

We covered our tracks by wading up the now swollen river, and set a course due west, not knowing that the Taungnyo range of mountains ran in an unbroken line south of Moulmein. At first we made reasonable headway, covering about 4 kilometres a day and taking turns to lead, forcing a path through dense undergrowth. Our routine varied little. A morning meal of soggy boiled rice, a short rest at midday, but no food, and on again until about 5.00 p.m. Initially we tried to erect some form of shelter for the night, as the rain was incessant, and those not doing this would collect wood for a fire. Lighting a fire in such wet conditions was not easy, but once burning we kept it alight all night to ward off tigers. However, our chief fear was not of animals, or even of deadly tree snakes, but of the ever-present leeches which got inside our clothes and had to be burnt off, while we still had matches.

We ran into hilly country, and soon the jungle became so dense with fallen interlocking bamboos that we were lucky to cover half a kilometre a day. There were no edible berries, but I tried eating fungus, assuming that anything poisonous would make me vomit.

On 25 July we were down to our last rice, three days later shared one small tin of pilchards between the ten of us, and four days after that we suffered our first casualty. Brown could not be found in the morning. For the last few days he had been very ill with gangrenous tropical ulcers, and had become delirious. Being so cold and wet at night, we were frequently getting up to relieve ourselves and stoke the fire, so with the constant movement his departure was unnoticed. He must have had great courage to 'walk out' instead of being a liability to us. We searched for him back along the track, but dared not waste too much of our dwindling strength, so had to implement our agreement and go on without him.

This took a great toll on us psychologically because, in our hearts, we knew this would not be an isolated case. Indeed, on 2 August Jack Feathers died during the night, having become very thin and troubled by swollen feet. Then, on 5 August Wilkie died shortly after making camp in the evening, presumably from heart failure, as we had encountered some of the steepest gradients of our journey. He was a big man and the excessive loss of weight proved too much for him. I felt Wilkie's death more than any other; he had been a true friend to me and I was privileged to have served under such a fine man.

Robbie and Jones were our next casualties. Jones fell unconscious, and we carried him until we found an old hunters' hut by a tributary of the Ye. In this hut Robbie died from septicaemia and dysentery, and that same night Jones begged us to go on and leave him, as he was unable to move. We tried to make him comfortable and left him with a full water bottle, knowing that this brave man would never be seen alive again.

On 14 August we reached the wide and slow-moving River Ye, the point for which we had been aiming. It was so good to be out of the dense jungle and to see the sky for the first time. We decided to use our last strength to cut bamboo for a raft, a task which took us three days, with our slow, laboured movements. We were all, by now, down to half our normal weight. Ian Moffat's legs were in a terrible state, with maggot-filled tropical ulcers from his thighs to his ankles. On completion of the raft, lashed together with strips of blanket, we set off down river. Our progress was short-lived, however, as the river turned sharply west and we saw in front of us a narrow gorge with tremendous rapids. The raft was totally smashed and we lost practically everything.

We managed to reach the bank, and met the first human beings we had seen since leaving Sonkurai, two Burmese hunters who took us to their hut and gave us food, our first for three weeks. At this point our troubles really began. The following day, 18 August, we met the headman of Karni *kampong* and over the next few days were displayed to the curious but kindly local villagers. However, we never trusted the headman of Karni, whom we suspected of having sold us to the Japanese for a large reward, and this proved to be so.

On 21 August Japanese troops, accompanied by Burmese police, arrested us and took us by boat to the Japanese HQ at Ye, where we were individually questioned for three days. This was civilised interrogation compared with what was to come at the hands of the *Kempeitai* (Military Police). On 24 August we travelled by train, locked in two filthy lavatories, from Ye to Moulmein, a journey of about 140 kilometres. After a night in a cage in the *Kempeitai* HQ we were taken to Moulmein Civilian Gaol, where we stayed until 5 September. Nur Mahommed was now parted from us and we never saw him again during hostilities.

Our party was reduced to four: Bill Anker, Ian Moffat, Guy Machado and myself. Handcuffed in pairs, the Japanese decided to parade us at various camps on the railway, as a deterrent to any would-be escapees. We remained at one camp, Kami Sonkurai, for two weeks. This was just north of Sonkurai Camp 2, from where we had originally escaped, and here we endured hard and prolonged interrogation. Hitherto, no-one had ever crossed the mountainous jungle between the Three Pagodas Pass and the coast of Tavoy. They suspected, I believe, that we were parachutists, which probably explains why they didn't kill us on arrest, as had happened to others.

We were returned, on 24 September, to Moulmein Gaol to await the completion of the railway, and on 5 October were again collected by the Moulmein *Kempeitai* to start our second journey south. Four days later, at Sonkurai Camp 2, we were told that we were to be taken to Nieke, the F Force HQ camp, for execution that afternoon. I felt that death by firing squad might almost be preferable to our existence at that time, although my determination to return to my family had in no way diminished.

Senior British officers, among whom was Cyril Wild, were brought to Nieke to witness our execution. With his usual quick appreciation of the situation, Cyril acted immediately and warned Col Banno of the everlasting disgrace his action would bring upon the Emperor and the Imperial Japanese Army if he personally allowed the executions to take place.

This episode is best described by Cyril himself, in a report he wrote after our court-martial at Raffles College, the Japanese 7th Army Area

Headquarters in Singapore, on 26 June 1944, almost ten months after our recapture:

Trial of Anker, Bradley, Moffat and Machado

These four officers escaped from F Force in Thailand in July 1943. I was warned by Col Banno's headquarters to hold myself in readiness to go to Nieke Camp and see them shot on their recapture. With permission of Lt-Col S.W. Harris, OBE, RA, Senior British officer of F Force, I saw Col Banno, who said that these officers had deserted their men in trouble. I replied that, on the contrary, the Japanese having made it impossible for them to look after their men, and being themselves unwilling to see them die by hundreds, they had been prepared to risk their own lives in an attempt to escape to India and let the British Army and the outside world know how the Japanese treated their prisoners on the Thailand railway. I also told Col Banno that when we left Singapore we were told to trust in the Imperial Japanese Army and no harm would come to us. Three months later, 1,700 of those who had trusted in the Imperial Japanese Army were dead and hundreds more were dying. At this Lt-Col Banno rather surprisingly started to weep.

To do him justice, it appears that he did prevent these four from being executed, and although they were given 8/9 years' imprisonment they were all brought out from Outram Prison on grounds of ill health after two or three months, and did not serve the rest of their sentences.

When these four officers were imprisoned at Sonkurai camp on recapture, before being sent to Singapore for court-martial, I managed to tell them that their only line of defence must be that which I had taken with Banno. As expected, the Japanese tried to impute motives of cowardice and self-interest to them, but all four stuck to this line of defence, coupled with a strenuous attack in court on the conditions on the Thailand railway. (This was confirmed recently by Furuta, the interpreter.) In spite of this, the Jap court-martial summary shows that they were sentenced on trumped-up charges, which put their motives for escape in a very poor light.

From this report I pick out these words: 'To do him justice, it appears that he (Col Banno) did prevent these four from being executed'. This is typical of Cyril, to take no credit for himself, but there can be no doubt that it was Cyril alone who saved our lives.

Subsequently he found a summary of our trial, giving the names of the three judges and that of the interpreter, Hiroyuki Furuta. In keeping with Japanese legal tradition, the sentences were decided beforehand and there was no defending officer. The charge against me ran as follows:

The accused, Bradley, was isolated at that time at the detached place in Sonkurai, under suspicion of keeping in him cholera germs, and the fear for cholera drove him to bitter home-sick, when he was urged by above-mentioned Wilkinson, at the end of June 1943, to join his decamping party. Acceding to this request, he ran away from the camp, together with other members of the party, and was apprehended by the Japanese Garrison in the same manner as Anker.

Having sentenced us to 8/9 years' hard labour, which meant solitary confinement, the Presiding Judge, Major Yoshiharu Ōmomo, gave us each a small bag of sweets and told us to take 'the greatest care of our health'! The summary of our trial ended with these words: 'The execution of penal servitude was suspended on 19 August 1945'.

Cyril's report on F Force continues:

> By the end of July the position of the Force was desperate. Communication between the camps and either Burma or Thailand had ceased, owing to impassable roads and broken bridges; 1,800 of the Force had died. In one camp alone the following diseases were prevalent: cholera, typhus, spinal meningitis, smallpox, diphtheria, jaundice, pneumonia, pleurisy, malaria, dysentery, scabies, beri-beri and tropical ulcers. With the exception of quinine, there were very few drugs and no dressings available throughout the whole area, and hideous tropical ulcers were dressed with banana leaves and puttees, or with dressings improvised from old shorts or shirts. The result was that some 70 amputations of limbs were necessary, entirely due to lack of dressings and because the men suffering from ulcers had been forced out to work by the Japanese. Deaths in one camp alone (Sonkurai) were then averaging 12 a day, and of the original 1,600 British troops who marched into that camp in May, 1,200 were dead before December.

Amputations on the railway had to be carried out with little or no anaesthetic, the only instruments available being saws, so very few patients survived. At one camp the Japanese engineers would lend their saw on condition it was cleaned properly before being returned. The operations were usually performed under a mosquito net, but sometimes in the open with an orderly fanning to keep the flies away. There being no catgut for sutures, black thread unravelled from clothing was used. Nearly all containers and utensils in the 'hospitals' as well as in the camps were made out of bamboo, and medical records were kept on slivers of bamboo. Sharpened spoons were sometimes used for removing putrid flesh from tropical ulcers. The pain can be imagined.

For cholera, all the doctors could do was to inject a saline solution made from rock salt and boiled creek water. This was done with improvised cannulas made from the rubber tubes of stethoscopes and hollow bamboo needles.

The native coolies suffered terribly, with no medical attention at all. When too ill to work they were driven out into the jungle to die and, in certain instances, they were buried or burned before they were dead. Over 10,000 coolies died on the railway.

The medical officers received more frequent beatings than anyone, except the interpreters. The interpreters for intervening in disputes, usually arising out of language difficulties, and the doctors for trying to prevent sick men from being taken out on working parties, were frequently cuffed, beaten, kicked, and on more than one occasion wounded by irate Japanese and Koreans. There was no amelioration in these conditions until the railway was completed and the force was withdrawn from the jungle.

H Force, consisting of 2,669 men when they left Changi, were more fortunate than F Force, as their sector was further south, between F Force and Banpong. Their line of communication was shorter and better and, as a result, they lost fewer men. However, no-one had an easy life on the railway and conditions were appalling for everyone.

Except possibly for their treatment of the Chinese in Malaya, with those mass executions of 1942, the Burma-Siam railway is arguably the blackest mark on the Japanese record in South-East Asia, although horrifying conditions existed in all Far-Eastern prisoner-of-war and civilian internment camps, and all had their stories of atrocities to tell. Primarily responsible for it was complete organisational ineptitude on the part of the Japanese. Coolies and prisoners-of-war were dispatched in increasing numbers without any preparations being made for receiving them or keeping them supplied.

The railway was supposed to be completed before the monsoon of 1943. As it fell behind schedule, pressure from above increased and drove the engineers to make ever more exacting demands on their workers. The general attitude of the Japanese was based not only on the alleged decree of the Emperor (See page 44), but also on the assumption that prisoners-of-war had no rights. They held that any rights had been forfeited by the capitulation at Singapore. An exasperated British officer once said to Colonel Banno: 'How on earth do you expect to get away with this after the war?' 'A victorious Japan', Banno replied, 'will not have to answer questions.' Banno adhered to the fiction that the prisoners were receiving the same rations and treatment as the Japanese engineers. When a bullock was killed at a camp half would go to the 50 odd guards and the other half, including the bony parts, would be given to the 1,100 or 1,200 prisoners.

The wanton behaviour of the Japanese and Korean officers and men is ascribed by the more detached survivors not so much to any innate cruelty in the Japanese race, for men can be made into anything, good or bad, but to the intensive and successful efforts of the Japanese Army to brutalise and dehumanise those who entered its ranks. And there were a few Japanese – a very few – who did try to help a little. It is probable that the Japanese officers at the top and the leaders in Japan did not know what was going on. Whether they knew or not, the responsibility and the guilt rested largely with them. The Japanese people, of course, heard and knew nothing of these crimes.

It seemed to me, as a prisoner, that the Japanese guards were susceptible to their surroundings. In Singapore, which was a civilised city, we were not too badly treated, but in the jungle camps they seemed to lose their veneer of civilisation. They felt disgruntled and down-trodden and, indeed, had perhaps lost face in being given inferior jobs instead of fighting in the front line. In other words, they were second-class soldiers, and they thus took out their revengeful aggression on the prisoners who were, in their eyes having surrendered, beneath contempt. The Koreans, whose country was subjugated by the Japanese, had been incorporated into the lowest echelons of the Japanese army, even given Japanese names, and were now only too pleased to find a species of humanity subservient to themselves whom they could beat and kick. This was, perhaps, the main reason for their sadistic cruelty, and they certainly gave full vent to their pent-up hostility. Tōyama, a notorious Korean at Sonkurai, used to wield a steel-shafted golf club, a 'niblick', and he once split open the heads of two officers. He was the man who, at Kami Sonkurai in September 1943, told me and my fellow escapees, with obvious relish, that we were to be executed. Cyril's report concludes:

By the end of December, when the remnants of F Force arrived back in Singapore, more than 3,000 men had died out of the original 7,000 who had set out in April, and 1,000 had been left behind in Burma or Thailand, either as sick, incapable of surviving the journey, or as medical and administrative personnel in charge of them. Of the 3,000 survivors who returned to Singapore, 95% were heavily infected with malaria, 80% were suffering from general debility, and 50% required hospital treatment for a long period, chiefly through dysentery, beri-beri, chronic malaria, skin-disease and malnutrition. Six weeks after their return two Japanese medical officers examined these 3,000 survivors, with a view to selecting men for further work on aerodrome construction. They could find 125, fit for light duty only.

The events narrated here took place, not in the comparative security of a permanent POW camp, but in the remoteness of the Thailand jungle, and at the hands of a callous and vindictive enemy; they persisted over a long period, to which at the time no end could be foreseen except the likelihood of death by starvation, ill-treatment and disease. Here was no heat and excitement of war, and yet the hardships and privations endured by all were as bad as any likely to be met with on active service and the casualties were, unfortunately, at least as great.

In these conditions, the unbroken spirit of the Force, and the steady devotion to duty of many officers, NCOs and men, themselves often seriously ill, were indeed remarkable.

Captain Cyril H. D. Wild
(Ox. & Bucks L I)

Cyril was in charge of the last party of two to three hundred POWs to leave Sonkurai to return to Singapore. They travelled standing up, 57 to a truck, as far as Nieke. This was not a long distance, but if troop trains were passing on their way north, the POWs would be shunted into a siding, often for long periods of time, before continuing their journey south to Kanchanaburi. At this camp officers were segregated from their men, and Cyril remained here for three weeks with the officers of H Force. On his return to Singapore he lived with these same officers in Changi for the rest of the war.

We got back to Changi in December 1943, and after that there is really little to say: for things were never too bad at Changi, although we were hungry for the last six months on a daily ration of 6 oz. rice, 2 oz. maize, 2 oz. or a little more of vegetables, and about a spoonful of whitebait! I was down to 9st 10 lb. at the end, but I kept amazingly fit all through and never suffered from either malaria or dysentery, even in Thailand.

Cyril received, personally, in three and a half years, the equivalent of one and a half food parcels of the type which POWs in Europe expected to receive weekly.

It seems fitting to end this chapter with the rondeau that Cyril wrote in Singapore in June 1944:

SONKURAI LABOUR CAMP
(Thailand Railway 1943)
Qui ante diem perierunt

At Sonkurai, where hope lay drowned
Beneath the bridge, the earth is browned
　　With mould, sad monsoon-vapours veil
　　The jungle, and the creepers trail
Like snakes inert, their coils unwound.

And there our rear-guard keep their ground
(Eight comrades laid beneath each mound),
　　A thousand, dead without avail,
　　At Sonkurai.

Freed from the captive's weary round,
Homeless, a lasting home they found.
  Let not our faith their courage fail,
  Till with the dawn the stars turn pale
And (silent long) our bugles sound
  At Sonkurai!

NOTES

[1] Lt Wakabayashi

[2] The engineer officer in charge of Sonkurai was Lt Hiroshi Ābe, who was conspicuous at all times in failing to stop brutal treatment by his men, even in his presence. Lt Ābe was ultimately sentenced to death, but the sentence was commuted to 15 years.

[3] This direct access was obtained with the cooperation of Lt Wakabayashi.

[4] Capt. Tsuneo Fukuda was ultimately sentenced to death, but this sentence was commuted to life.

Chapter 5
JAPANESE SURRENDER

Early in August 1945 there was a marked change in the attitude of the guards at Changi; they tended to become either more truculent and irrational, or more obsequious. This, coupled with the now more openly available radio news gave hope to all, but how would the camp guards react when the end came, as surely it must?

The blockade of the Japanese mainland and islands by US submarines was bringing economic defeat, preventing the exploitation of Japan's new territories. The Japanese Navy was completely crippled, and incessant air strikes were bringing home to the Japanese people the truth that they could no longer hope to defend their country.

The Potsdam Declaration had been presented to Japan on 26 July 1945 by the three major Allies – China, Great Britain and the United States. There were four basic demands:

1. Demobilisation of Japanese armed forces.

2. Allied occupation of Japan.

3. Elimination 'for all time those who have deceived and misled the people of Japan.'

4. Trial of Japanese war criminals by an Allied tribunal. 'Stern justice shall be meted out to all war criminals, including those who have visited cruelties upon our prisoners.'

It warned that Japan must surrender or face 'utter destruction' and added: 'Japan shall be given an opportunity to end the war.'

Japan chose to ignore Potsdam; in the word of Prime Minister Suzuki, *mokusatsu*, to kill it with silence. President Truman, faced with the prospect of invading Japan, with the resulting loss of millions of lives, authorised the dropping of the atomic bomb. On 6 August the first one completely destroyed Hiroshima. The Emperor, as he stood on a hill overlooking the city, is reputed to have commented, 'There seems to have been considerable damage here.' Hirohito sent a message to the Prime

Minister saying the war must end, but the cabinet remained reluctant to take action. Three days later a second atomic bomb was dropped on Nagasaki, sealing Japan's fate, for on the same day Russia declared war, marched into Manchuria and met little opposition.

At this point the Emperor intervened and called an immediate meeting of his council in the imperial bunker. The war minister and the army and navy chiefs-of-staff continued to be adamant that there should be a suicidal last battle, but in an unprecedented move Emperor Hirohito *spoke*. He called for the acceptance of the Potsdam Declaration and, by so doing, agreed to the Allied demand to dispense 'stern justice' to Japan's war criminals.

> It goes without saying that it is unbearable for me to see the brave and loyal fighting men of Japan disarmed. It is equally unbearable that others who have rendered me devoted service should now be punished as instigators of the war. Nevertheless, the time has come when we must bear the unbearable...

Thus the Allies were notified that Japan was prepared to surrender, provided it was agreed that the Imperial Institution should be maintained. It was unthinkable that Japan's god-emperor could be arraigned in the dock as a war criminal. General MacArthur acquiesced to respect the wishes of the Japanese people, a concession which, one now realises, prevented any leanings towards communism. The people of Japan, however, knew nothing of the decision to surrender, and it was the Emperor himself who said he wished to make a broadcast to the nation. At a second imperial conference on 14 August he acknowledged that Japan was defeated and would be destroyed if the war continued. He would not permit that to happen, regardless of the consequences to himself.

> As the people of Japan are unaware of the present situation, I know they will be deeply shocked when they hear of our decision. If it is thought appropriate that I explain the matter to them personally, I am willing to go before the microphone... I desire the cabinet to prepare as soon as possible an Imperial Rescript announcing the termination of the war.

Conservative Japanese were horrified at the idea of the Emperor speaking directly to his people, so it was arranged that a recording should be made. This was done on the evening of 14 August, but military extremists tried unsuccessfully to find and destroy the recording. The broadcast went out as planned on 15 August, explaining that 'the war has not progressed necessarily in our favour' and describing the enemy's 'new and most cruel bomb'. He added, 'Should we continue to fight, not only would it result in an ultimate collapse and obliteration of the Japanese nation, but also it would lead to the total extinction of human civilisation.' The Emperor's prestige and personal intervention sufficed to bring an orderly transition to peace.

The answer to the fate of all prisoners-of-war and civilians in Japanese hands had the war continued became clear from a document produced at the subsequent trial of General Hideki Tōjō:

INTERNATIONAL PROSECUTION SECTION
BRITISH DIVISION

Document No. 2701 (Certified as Exhibit 'O' in Doc. No. 2687)

From the Journal of the Taiwan POW Camp HQ in Taihoku, entry 1 August 1944

1. (not applicable)

2. The following answer about the extreme measures for POWs was sent to the Chief-of-Staff of the 11th Unit (Formosa POW Security No. 10).

'Under the present situation if there were a mere explosion or fire a shelter for the time being could be had in nearby buildings such as the school, a warehouse, or the like. However, at such time as the situation became urgent and it be extremely important, the POWs will be concentrated and confined in their present location and under heavy guard the preparation for the final disposition will be made. The time and method of this disposition are as follows:

(1) *The Time*
Although the basic aim is to act under superior orders, individual disposition may be made in the following circumstances:

(a) When an uprising of large numbers cannot be suppressed without the use of firearms.

(b) When escapers from the camp may turn into a hostile fighting force.

(2) *The Methods*

(a) Whether they are destroyed individually or in groups, or however it is done, with mass bombing, poisonous smoke, poisons, drowning, decapitation, or what, dispose of them as the situation dictates.

(b) In any case it is the aim not to allow the escape of a single one, to annihilate them all, and not to leave any traces.

(3) To: The Commanding General... Taiwan POW Camps'.

I hereby certify that this is a true translation from the Journal of the Taiwan POW HQ in Taiwan, entry 1 August 1944.

signed: Stephen H. Green

This is Exhibit marked 'O' referred to in the Affidavit of James Thomas Nehemiah Cross,

Sworn before me this 19th day of September 1946.

signed: P.A.L. Vine
Major, RM

Lieutenant Cross, 80th Anti-Tank Regt, RA, was Adjutant to Major J.F. Crossley, RA, at Kinkaseki camp, Taiwan.

Similar directives were in force in all Japanese or occupied territories. Indeed, POWs in many camps were made to dig large trenches – mass graves for themselves. As stated in the above document, had an Allied landing taken place there would have been a total massacre of all surviving prisoners-of-war and civilian internees, including women and children.

There was, in fact, a landing on the Japanese mainland planned for November 1945, with a further landing designated for March 1946. If these had taken place the casualties on both sides would have been horrendous. Japan was prepared to sacrifice millions in the defence of her homeland, and General MacArthur and Admiral Nimitz expected almost a million casualties, including wounded, in mounting such an attack. By dropping the two atomic bombs 170,000 died at Hiroshima and Nagasaki, but half that number of civilians and POWs were saved, together with the millions of casualties that would have resulted from the assault on Japan; and it must not be forgotten that the victorious Allied troops from the west, having so recently celebrated VE Day in Europe, would inevitably have been drawn into the Far-Eastern conflict.

General MacArthur insisted that he personally must take the Japanese surrender in Tokyo on 2 September, before surrenders could be accepted in the outlying territories. The time gap from 15 August to 2 September was unfortunate as it enabled the Japanese militarists to destroy tons of war records, valuable evidence of war criminality. There were bonfires at War Ministry offices on Ichigaya Hill, at army and navy installations throughout the Japanese territories and at the headquarters of the *Kempeitai* (Military Police). Not only did the surrender interval give time to destroy documents, it also provided the chance to falsify records. Both these factors were detrimental to the war crimes trials that were to follow, but fortunately not all incriminating documents were burnt.

It was known that prisoners-of-war everywhere were in the last stages of malnutrition and in fear of their lives from vengeful guards and, although nothing could be done officially before that date, in practice aid was parachuted into many of the camps.

On 28 August Allied aircraft dropped leaflets over Changi, one side addressed to the Japanese, bearing instructions on how to treat prisoners-of-war, and the other side addressed to the prisoners themselves:

TO ALL ALLIED PRISONERS-OF-WAR
THE JAPANESE FORCES HAVE SURRENDERED
UNCONDITIONALLY AND THE WAR IS OVER

WE will get supplies to you as soon as is humanly possible and will make arrangements to get you out but, owing to the distances involved, it may be some time before we can achieve this.

YOU will help us and yourselves if you act as follows:

(1) Stay in your camp until you get further orders from us.

(2) Start preparing nominal rolls of personnel giving fullest particulars.

(3) List your most urgent necessities.

(4) If you have been starved or under fed for long periods DO NOT eat large quantities of solid food, fruit or vegetables at first. It is dangerous for you to do so. Small quantities at frequent intervals are much safer and will strengthen you far more quickly. For those who are really ill or very weak, fluids such as broth and soup, making use of the water in which rice and other foods have been boiled, are much the best. Gifts of food from the local population should be cooked. We want to get you back home quickly, safe and sound, and we do not want to risk your chances from diarrhoea, dysentery and cholera at this last stage.

(5) Local authorities and/or Allied officers will take charge of your affairs in a very short time. Be guided by their advice.

On 30 August the first Allied troops arrived in Changi. Two doctors and an orderly were dropped by parachute, bringing with them limited supplies of drugs, and on 5 September troops of the 5th Indian Division landed and started to take the Japanese into custody. Admiral Lord Louis Mountbatten, Supreme Allied Commander South-East Asia, requested that Lady Mountbatten should come to advise on the prisoner-of-war repatriation, because 'she *really* does know her stuff and can help'.

Already in March and April of 1945 Edwina Mountbatten had worked selflessly, exhausting the people who accompanied her, on a tour that covered 34,000 miles. She later put herself in dangerous situations, as she often operated in areas ahead of the Allied forces, where she could have come across dissident Japanese reluctant to surrender. A few hours after the liberation she and Admiral Mountbatten visited Changi Gaol together and, indeed, whenever Admiral Mountbatten had a spare moment he joined his wife and, between them, they visited every camp in the Singapore area and all the hospitals, speaking to as many people as possible. I was one of those privileged to meet Lady Edwina, as she visited me on a hospital ship before I left for home.

It was obviously of prime importance to get the POWs and internees home as soon as possible, and many of them alive today remember Lady Edwina with great affection. Her efficiency, however, presented Cyril with a problem in that he had very little time in which to collect evidence against war criminals before everyone departed!

Inevitably, there were areas where the Japanese had to be used to maintain order in the camps, even after the surrender, but they tended to slip away and there were few about. Philip Ziegler, in his book, *Mountbatten – The Official Biography*, writes: 'He (Mountbatten) insisted that in his zone swords should be surrendered by all senior officers in formal ceremonies in front of their men, and distributed the spoils among his own officers and selected beneficiaries at home.' Cyril was one of those officers to be given a Japanese sword – none other than that belonging to General Yamashita, which was appropriate as he had encountered him at the Allied surrender, and was to meet him again when he personally interrogated him in Manila before his trial.

Cyril wrote:

> I was able to start in right away when we were relieved at the end of August. For two weeks before that the Japs had been doing pretty well what we told them. But after a Canadian called Lt-Col Stewart arrived from Johore, having parachuted into the Chinese guerrillas' area in the jungle, I joined up with him and life began again.

Although by no means 100% fit after his three and a half years as a prisoner, Cyril remained behind to use his invaluable knowledge and experience during the initial work of starting war crimes investigations in South-East Asia. With his unique knowledge of the Japanese language he was able to discover through personal interrogation the truth about many atrocities, which might well have remained a mystery for all time. To do this he sacrificed an early return to his wife, whom he had not seen for so long.

Major-General M.D. Price, CB, OBE, recalled in the Journal of the Royal Signals Institution of summer 1981:

> By the time parts of Force 136 emerged from the jungle a day or so later it had become obvious that better communications were needed within the camp to organise repatriation, and I was ordered to set up an exchange and telephones. So it was that I found myself at a meeting presided over by a Lieutenant-Colonel of Force 136, an ex-Vancouver policeman (Lt-Col

69

Bob Stewart), with the Senior British Officer and a number of Japanese to inform them of our various requirements. Our interpreter, Cyril Wild, spoke the most beautiful Japanese and had interpreted for General Percival at Singapore's surrender. He insisted that the Japanese interpreter should do the work, but found it necessary to interrupt at intervals with the gentle remark, "That was not quite what the colonel said, was it?", as the Canadian did not mince his words and the little man had never had to speak to a senior Japanese officer in anything like those terms before. Eventually he was reduced to silent tears, rose from the table and vanished, to what fate we never knew.

Cyril:

It was great fun talking to the Japs from the right end of the table at last, especially to Major-General Saitō, formerly in charge of all POWs and internees in Malaya and Sumatra, whom we have since gaoled. I spent a good part of the four days *prior* to the first landing by our troops in touring the island in a fine roadster commandeered from a Jap general, with a large Union Jack flying on the radiator, recceing all the aerodromes and demanding and getting salutes from all Jap guards. On 5 September a Major Cooper (an aerodrome engineer flown in by Mosquito from the Cocos Islands) and I were driving through Singapore from one of the western aerodromes and were surprised by the tumultuous cheers which greeted us in every street, particularly wherever there were any disconsolate Japs about! The explanation came when we reached the dock-area, and met the first of the landing-troops advancing cautiously from block to block – Indian troops in their (to me) still unfamiliar jungle-green. We drove down to the dockside where we met Major-General Mansergh, GOC 5th Indian Division, whose first words were to tell us to take the Union Jack off our car – quite politely, and quite rightly, of course, as only a C-in-C is entitled to fly it! But I thought that this was quite the funniest of my several flag-adventures; after living under the Rising Sun for $3^{1}/_{2}$ years in Singapore, to be told, by the first British General to land there, to pull down the Union Jack! Next day I moved with Col Stewart from Changi to the Goodwood Park Hotel, where his outfit, E Group, an Intelligence branch of Supreme Allied Commander South-East Asia, were setting up an Advance HQ. E Group's job was to be War Crimes, but after a day or two they were all diverted to work for Mastiff, i.e. the branch of RAPWI (returned Allied prisoners-of-war and internees), supplying and evacuating by air all POWs and internees in Java, Sumatra, etc., apparently under the direct orders of that very efficient staff-officer, Lady Louis Mountbatten. The result was that for three hectic weeks I found myself handling *all* the War Criminals and Atrocities business for Malaya, part-Thailand, Sumatra, Borneo, etc. etc. during the really critical stage when RAPWI and Mastiff were evacuating everyone as fast as they could, and the evidence *had* to be collected and collated before they went.

To help me I had *no* officers and about one-third interest in a rather unwilling clerk. However, I got it and did it so far as the 50 or so really major atrocities were concerned, and the rest can wait, for every single individual who has been a prisoner or internee of the Japs has at least one perfectly genuine atrocity-story to tell, either at first or second hand. By major atrocities I mean episodes such as the burning alive with petrol of a hundred Australian and fifty Indian wounded in Johore; the marching into the sea, machine-gunning and bayonetting of 30 Australian nurses; and the *cold-blooded* murder of 200 Medical officers, Orderlies and wounded at Alexandra Hospital, including our friend Dr Allardyce, who was our doctor in Kôbe; – and others, worse than these, which I prefer not to repeat. It has been worth 12/15 hours work a day since release. For if I had not done it, there was *no-one* to take my place. Besides, I have a wider knowledge of these matters, probably, than anyone. I have handled a lot of these cases at the time: I have been the recipient of countless stories in captivity from victims of ill-treatment: I can identify a large number of the criminals, and when I interrogate them they dare not lie because I know the facts.

I have, in fact, made many of the arrests myself, and done most of the interrogation, in addition to grappling with the enormous documentary side. For this I am some sort of a GSO2(I), and at least I have the satisfaction of emerging from captivity into the same style of job which I had before; and I shall go home as a soldier from a campaign, and not as an ex-POW.[1]

The official surrender of Japanese forces in South-East Asia took place on 12 September 1945 in the Council Chamber of the Municipal Buildings at Singapore. The ceremony was attended by almost every senior officer in the area, including representatives of the Empire and of many Allied countries. Cyril was present at the invitation of Admiral Mountbatten.

The guard of honour was mounted on the space before the buildings by detachments from the Royal Navy, the RAF Regiment, Australian parachute troops, and Dogras from the 5th Division, while 400 naval ratings, several hundred Indian troops, and airmen formed three sides of the outer square.

Distant cheering and clapping preceded the arrival of the Supreme Allied Commander and his deputy, Lieutenant-General Wheeler, who arrived in an open car and were welcomed by the three Commanders-in-Chief, Lieutenant-General Sir William Slim (commanding the Allied Land Forces in South-East Asia), Admiral Sir Arthur Power (Commander-in-Chief, East Indies Fleet), and Air Marshal Sir Keith Park (commanding the Allied Air Forces in South-East Asia).

Fifty men of the 1st Battalion of the West Yorkshire Regiment were on parade, and during the inspection flights of Mosquitoes, Sunderlands and Dakotas flew low overhead. Sixty-one warships lay in harbour as a background of naval strength. These included the *Nelson* and *Richelieu*, the cruisers *Sussex* (the first to enter Singapore after the capitulation), *Cumberland, Royalist* and *Ceylon*, five escort-carriers and eight destroyers. Before the inspection was over a noise in the crowd signified the arrival of the Japanese party. Admiral Mountbatten entered the building past the Marine guards on the steps.

The Council Chamber was a large room with balcony and marble columns, and on one wall hung a large portrait of King George VI, recently recovered from Raffles Museum. Two long tables were drawn up at which the 12 Allied representatives were to sit, facing the seven Japanese. The distinguished assembly from many nations included General Carton de Wiart, who had elected to be present rather than attend the Nanking surrender, General Dempsey, the new Commander-in-Chief of the Fourteenth Army, the Sultan of Johore, the Maharaja of Cooch Behar, a representative of the Netherlands East Indies Government, Sir Archibald Rowlands, General Sir Philip Christison, the Right Reverend Leonard Wilson, Bishop of Singapore, ten other internees, twelve Chinese representatives and other local figures. Space was also found for a few prisoners-of-war and members of the Chinese guerrilla forces.

At 11 a.m. the Japanese filed in, led by Brigadier Rogers. They were General Itagaki, commanding the Seventh Area Army (Malaya, Java and Sumatra), Lieutenant-General Numata, chief of staff to Count Terauchi, the Japanese Supreme Commander, Lieutenant-General Nakamura, commanding the Eighteenth Area Army (Siam), Lieutenant-General Kimura, commanding the Burma Area Army, Lieutenant-General Kinoshita, commanding the Third Army, with headquarters at Singapore, Vice-Admiral Fukutomi, commanding the First Southern Expeditionary Fleet, based on Singapore, and Vice-Admiral Shibata, commanding the Second Southern Expeditionary Fleet, based on Surabaya. They wore khaki uniform, white shirts with open collars and many ribbons, including some Allied ones from the first world war, but of course no swords, as these had already been surrendered. The admirals were in long trousers, the generals in boots and spurs, and they all looked weary, disillusioned old men. They remained standing until Admiral Mountbatten entered, when everyone rose. He took his seat and motioned to the company to sit down.

Admiral Mountbatten began the proceedings by reading a telegram from the Japanese Supreme Commander, Count Terauchi, who was too ill to attend, appointing General Itagaki to sign on his behalf: 'In the circumstances', he said, 'I have decided to accept the surrender from General Itagaki today, but I have warned the field-marshal that I shall expect him to make his personal surrender to me as soon as he is fit enough to do so.' He went on to refer to the landings of British and Indian forces at Port Dickson and Port Swettenham.

'When I visited the beaches yesterday men were landing in an endless stream. As I speak there are 100,000 men ashore. This invasion would have taken place on 9 September, whether the Japanese had resisted or not. I wish to make this plain: the surrender today is no negotiated surrender; the Japanese are submitting to the superior force now massed here. I now call upon General Itagaki to produce his credentials.'

The instrument of surrender was read, and ten copies were taken to Itagaki to sign. He did this in Japanese characters, affixing both the official seal and his smaller personal seal to each one. They were then signed by Admiral Mountbatten before being distributed – one to the Japanese and the rest retained by the Allied Governments.

After the signing Admiral Mountbatten said quietly, 'I now ask the Japanese representatives kindly to withdraw.' Itagaki made a slight bow to the Supreme Commander, and they filed out with their escorts. It had been a solemn and dignified occasion, and particularly striking was the international character of the gathering, representatives of the many Allied countries whom the Japanese had contrived to array against them. Everyone was particularly glad that a distinguished representative of the Indian Army was present. Admiral Mountbatten then went out to the steps of the Municipal Buildings and read out the text of his order of the day:

> I have today received the surrender of the Supreme Commander of the Japanese forces who have been fighting the Allies, and I have accepted the surrender on behalf of all of you. I wish you all to know the deep pride I feel in every man and woman in the command today. You have inflicted on the Japanese six times the number of deaths that they have inflicted on you.
>
> The defeat of Japan in the last month is the first in history. For hundreds of years the Japanese have been ruled by a small set of imperialists, and they have been told to look upon themselves as a superior race of divine origin. They have been taught to be arrogant to foreigners and to believe that the treachery they practised at Pearl Harbour is a virtue so long as it ends in Japanese victory. They are finding it very hard to accept the defeat or try to wriggle out of the terms of surrender.
>
> Field-Marshal Count Terrauchi, the Supreme Commander of the Japanese forces in this area, is at the present time an ill man. He had a stroke last April, and I have therefore decided to accept the surrender through General Itagaki, though I have ordered that the field-marshal should report to me in person as soon as he is fit to travel. You may rest assured that I shall tolerate no evasion on the part of the Japanese.
>
> I am telling you this because I wish to warn you of the situation you may find when you proceed to liberate other territories in this command.

In the new territories you will be occupying the Japanese have not been beaten in battle. You may well find, therefore, that these Japanese who have not been beaten may still fanatically believe in the divine superiority of their race. They may try to behave arrogantly. You will have my support in taking the firmest measures against any Japanese obstinacy, impudence, or non-cooperation.

There is much more to be done. You will realise how much when I say that the enlarged South-East Asia Command now includes 1,500,000 square miles of land with a population of 128,000,000 people. For some months to come SEAC will have to undertake such vital tasks as the repatriation of prisoners-of-war and civilian internees who number 200,000 and have first claim on us. We have to remove 500,000 Japanese, feed them properly, give them work, and bring them back to peace-time conditions.

This will require a great deal of planning, hard work, initiative, and understanding. I feel assured that I can rely on you to do as well in peace as you did in war. In the meantime you will agree that our prisoners-of-war have suffered so much that they have the first call on our shipping.

The Union Jack was formally hoisted to its rightful position, while the Marine Band played 'God Save the King' and the anthems of America, China, Holland and France. This moment, for Cyril, must surely have been the most poignant of the whole occasion, for this very flag was the one that he had kept hidden, at great danger to himself, throughout the three and a half years of captivity. An article on the surrender ceremony in *The Times* of 13 September 1945 describes the story of this particular flag:

A curious story is attached to the Union Jack which was hoisted. The only officer present at today's ceremony who attended the surrender to Yamashita on 15 February 1942 was Major Cyril Wild, Oxfordshire and Buckinghamshire Light Infantry. He carried the flag of truce on that unhappy occasion and acted as interpreter. Brigadier Newbigging, of the Malaya Command, carried the Union Jack.[2] On returning to Fort Canning Major Wild collected the Union Jack and put it away. The Japanese later asked for it, but Major Wild told them that he had burned it on the ramparts of Fort Canning, looking towards England and his home, an answer which impressed them greatly.

Major Wild kept the flag and took it with him when he went into the prison camp. For two years it was used for funerals in the camp, only a handful of men knowing its history. The Japanese officer in charge of the camp later insisted that it should be given up, but it was still borrowed from him for funerals. At the time of Japan's surrender it was recovered and kept for an occasion such as this. It witnessed a great disaster to British arms; it has lain, as a final symbol of their country and calling, on the bodies of many brave men who died through the brutality or indifference of a callous foe, and today, though soiled and worn, it flutters proudly over Singapore, a symbol of a new and happier era.

Prior to the Allied surrender of Singapore the flag, which was to become famous and a focal point of international interest, flew in the equatorial sun above Fort Canning, the Malayan Command headquarters. Such a flag symbolised the continuity of British protection to the inhabitants of that island, that had been theirs since the Straits Settlements became a Crown Colony in 1867 and, indeed, a Union Jack had probably flown since the establishment of Singapore by Sir Stamford Raffles in 1819.

After the ceremony Admiral Lord Louis Mountbatten drove two miles back to his headquarters (and later wrote in his diary), 'through densely packed crowds to one never-ending thunderous wall of cheers... I think it is a remarkable demonstration of the delight of the people of Singapore to find the British back once more... To receive the unconditional surrender of half a million enemy soldiers, sailors and airmen must be an event which happens to few people in the world. I was very conscious that this was the greatest day of my life.' Lady Mountbatten found the ceremony 'quite the most impressive and moving I have ever seen.'

It must have been a great day too for the prisoners-of-war and internees attending the ceremony, representing thousands of people who had suffered for so long. Later that day Cyril made a broadcast over Singapore radio:

> The flag which has just been hoisted is the same Union Jack which the Japanese compelled us to carry at the British capitulation of Singapore on 15 February 1942. On that occasion I was with the British delegation which assisted General Percival.
>
> The emissaries received an order at the prisoner-of-war camp at Changi that I should hand over personally to the Japanese General Staff the Union Jack which had been used on that occasion.
>
> With General Percival's permission, I told the representatives of the Japanese General Staff that I had no flag to give them. I told them that I had personally burned the flag on the evening of the capitulation.
>
> As soon as we heard that the Potsdam Declaration had been accepted by the Japanese, we got out the flag and hoisted it on the flagstaff of the camp at Changi.
>
> Yesterday, I went to Government House, was received by the Supreme Commander, and I finally handed the flag over to one of his staff officers. Today I have been privileged to be a spectator at the surrender of the Japanese. During our long imprisonment we had been hoping that this day would come.

This short and very understated sentence at the end of the broadcast is indicative of how intensely moved Cyril must have been. The whole occasion, after so much suffering and privation endured so stoically by all surviving prisoners-of-war and internees, was charged with emotion.

Today, although many of the people have come and gone, this very flag remains as a lasting symbol of courage and endurance.

Meanwhile, Cyril's brother David, who had suffered five years as a German prisoner-of-war, was now liberated and back at home with his wife, Mary. He received a letter from Cyril, written on 8 October:

My dear David,

I have at last heard, in a letter from Celia which I got yesterday, that you are well and back at Eton with Mary. I cannot tell you what a joy it is to know this. It seemed so unlikely at times that all three of us (referring also to Maurice Waterhouse) would emerge safely from captivity, and knowing that you were in Poland I was most anxious about you after the fighting started there... Your three letters – the earliest of them about April '42 – all reached me: but of course I was never allowed to reply. They were a great help, and became an object of interest and envy to many – especially their *length*, when our ration was 25 words in 6/9 months. One thing which always comforted me about your situation was that your work went on as a prisoner and even became increasingly important: and I always knew what a tremendous help and comfort you must have been to hundreds, and perhaps thousands of men. Also you were able to stay with the men, which must have been a most stimulating trust and responsibility. I am sure, therefore, that you do not regard your five years as wasted – I know my mere three and a half were the most valuable I have ever spent, in many ways. But it has been a long parting...

NOTES

[1] Paper had been a rare and much valued commodity to prisoners-of-war. Every scrap was utilised to the full. This letter, handwritten by Cyril in small writing, with lines close together and few paragraphs, indicates that he was still in the habit of economising on paper.

[2] Brigadier Newbigging carried the Union Jack when first contact was made, but on the second occasion, when General Percival met General Yamashita, it was Brigadier K.S. Torrance, BGS Malaya Command, who carried the Union Jack.

ISLANDS OF THE RHIO AND LINGGA ARCHIPELAGOS

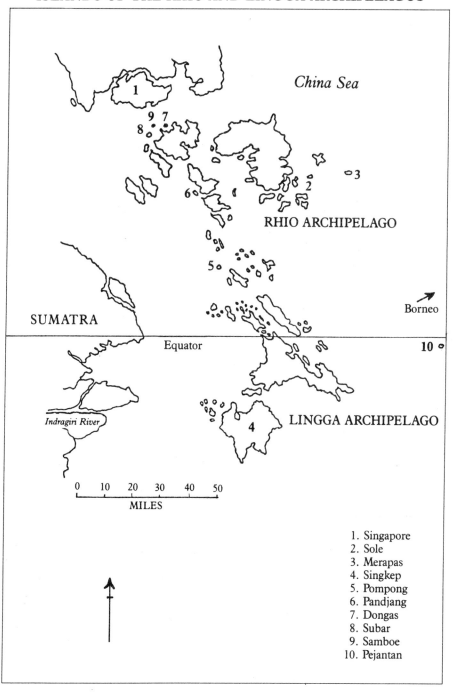

China Sea

RHIO ARCHIPELAGO

SUMATRA

Equator

Borneo

10 °

Indragiri River

LINGGA ARCHIPELAGO

0   10   20   30   40   50

MILES

1. Singapore
2. Sole
3. Merapas
4. Singkep
5. Pompong
6. Pandjang
7. Dongas
8. Subar
9. Samboe
10. Pejantan

Chapter 6

RIMAU

Three Christian crosses over three Chinese graves. This unlikely juxta-position, discovered just after he joined the War Crimes unit at the end of August 1945, aroused Cyril's curiosity and led him, eventually, to uncover the most incredible story.

It all began with Operation Jaywick, the brainchild of Captain Ivan Lyon who was educated at Harrow and, after attending the Royal Military College, Sandhurst, was commissioned into the Gordon Highlanders in 1935. Prior to the fall of Singapore he had been sent to help organise an escape route across Sumatra, via the Indragiri River, to Padang on the West coast, the port of embarkation for those attempting to reach Ceylon. His job had been to make caches of food on various islands to the south of Singapore, in the hope that they would save the lives of escapees making for Sumatra.

Captain Lyon, having completed his given task, finally reached Padang in the first week of March 1942. There he commandeered a large proa, the *Sederhana Johannes*, which he provisioned amply for an intended crossing of the Indian Ocean. He set sail, for the *Sederhana Johannes* had no engine, with a party of seventeen, all Europeans except for one Chinese and one Malay. Thirty-eight days after leaving Padang they were picked up by a freighter and taken to Colombo.

Here he heard that Bill Reynolds, an Australian who had served in destroyers in World War I, had escaped from Singapore in the *Kofuku Maru* and reached Bombay. These two men first met at the mouth of the Indragiri River, Sumatra, when they were both temporarily engaged in the same task of search and rescue of escapees from Singapore.

Even while recovering from the rigours of sailing across the Indian Ocean, Lyon was thinking of returning to Singapore to inflict the maximum damage possible on enemy shipping in Keppel Harbour. The *Kofuku Maru* was a Japanese fishing boat in British hands, and this seemed to him an invaluable aid to his proposed operation.

The *Kofuku Maru* was 78 feet long and 10 feet 6 inch beam, and she was like something one might see in any harbour in the world, drab and lacking in paint, but this very nonentity made her even more attractive to Lyon. She was Japanese built of solid teak, and boats of her type were common in South-East Asia. There is little doubt that the discovery of the *Kofuku Maru* encouraged Lyon to try and carry out what some thought was a hairbrained scheme.

Australia seemed the obvious base for his Operation Jaywick, as security would be much tighter in the approaches from nearer bases in Ceylon or India. Lyon, by now posted to a staff job in New Delhi, had cabled his wife, Gabrielle, to join him in India with their small son, Clive. She managed to get a passage on a ship from Perth but, tragically, her ship was torpedoed and she and Clive became prisoners of the Japanese. Meanwhile, Lyon had engineered his posting to Australia to organise Jaywick, and his second cable to Gabrielle arrived too late to prevent her fateful departure for India.

Lyon now threw himself relentlessly into getting together a party of volunteers for this operation. He was lucky in that he met Lieutenant D.M.N. Davidson, RNVR, educated at Cheltenham, followed by five years as a jackaroo, amongst other jobs, in Brisbane. He had returned to England and joined the Bombay Burma Trading Corporation which led him to the teak forests of Siam and Burma. Lyon knew immediately that he had found his second-in-command, and so his Jaywick force, to operate under the Inter-Allied Services Department, was born.

After roughly twelve months' intensive and gruelling training, the emphasis being on physical fitness, canoeing and the use of explosives, Lyon's force was ready for operations, the final number selected being thirteen. Meanwhile the *Kofuku Maru*, now renamed the *Krait* (meaning a deadly Indian rock snake), had been shipped as deck cargo on a British freighter and off-loaded in Sydney Harbour. Her moribund engine was later replaced by a Gardner Diesel, and number 4 hold was converted to an extra fuel tank, giving her a range of 13,000 miles with the extra 40 gallon drums on deck.

On 27 August 1943 the *Krait* reached Exmouth Gulf, Western Australia, where she took on four new type Folboats to replace the old training canoes. These were 17 feet long and 2 feet 6 inches wide, with three manholes in the deck, two for the crew and the third to hold the explosive charges, the limpets.

At 2.00 p.m. on 2 September the Blue Ensign was raised at the *Krait*'s stern, for Jaywick was an army operation, and that operation was now underway. The following morning Lyon spoke to all members of his group and told them of their objective. The whole scheme, so far, had been achieved in complete secrecy and so it would remain, by and large, until the end of the war. As it now became a seaborne operation Davidson assumed operational command.

On 18 September they reached Pandjang Island, about 30 miles south of Singapore, having buried a supply of food and water on Pompong Island, some 20 miles further from their target. It was agreed that the *Krait* would pick up the three canoe parties at midnight on 1 October, or failing that the *Krait* would make a final rendezvouz 48 hours later, before returning to Australia.

When all gear had been taken ashore the *Krait* headed back to the China Sea, leaving three officers, Lyon, Davidson and Page, with three ratings, Falls, Jones and Huston, to sort out and hide their stores.

At dusk on 20 September they launched their canoes and, dressed completely in black, they started paddling towards their target. During the daylight hours of the next two days they rested on uninhabited islands, and on 23 September landed on Dongas, a small jungle-covered island eight miles from Singapore. This was to be their forward observation post before the final attack, but the tide beat them and forced them to make their attack from Subar, where the current was less unfavourable.

On the night of 26 September, at 10.00 p.m., the three canoes came quietly and stealthily alongside their chosen targets, huge slab-sided hulks of Japanese freighters and tankers. They held their positions by attaching magnetic frames to the hulls of the ships, and positioned the limpits below the water line with the aid of broom handles. The fuses were set for five o'clock next morning, which gave them seven hours to make their escape. Lyon and Page reached Dongas at about 4.45 a.m., but there was no sign of Davidson who had decided to bypass Dongas and head straight to the pick-up point to hold back the *Krait*, if it should prove necessary. He and Falls reached Pompong twenty-three hours before the agreed rendezvous with the *Krait*.

At 3.00 a.m. on 2 October the other two canoes reached what they thought was the pick-up point at Pompong Island, but could find no sign of the *Krait*. They had, in fact, landed on the wrong beach, but were eventually picked up by the *Krait* at the second rendezvous. The excitement of the three raiding canoe crews can be imagined, as they heard the distant massive explosions signalling their success. What a sense of achievement the whole group must have felt, as they returned to Australia! Operation Jaywick was complete when the *Krait* arrived back at the American base of Potshot in Exmouth Gulf.

1. David and Cyril in 1912.
(The Very Revd J.H.S. Wild)

2. Patrick, Cyril, John and David, 1916.
(The Very Revd J.H.S. Wild)

3. The Bishop (*centre*) and his four sons at Benwell, Newcastle, in 1927, the year that Cyril left Charterhouse. (*left to right*) Patrick, Cyril, Bishop Wild, John and David.
(The Very Revd J.H.S. Wild)

4. Mount Nantai-San, Lake Chūzenji, Nikko. (Mrs. Mary Beazley)

5. Cyril fishing the Kisugawa river, Chūzenji, summer 1931.

(The Revd R.D.F. Wild)

6. Cyril (*left*) and his brother, David, best man at his wedding. St Giles Church, Oxford, 9 November 1935.

(The Very Revd J.H.S. Wild)

7. Cyril and Celia after their marriage at St Giles Church, Oxford, 9 November 1935.

8. The Surrender, 15 February 1942; the arrival at Ford Factory, Bukit Timah. On the extreme left, the rifle and bayonet of an IJA guard; *(left to right)* Capt. C.H.D. Wild (Ox. & Bucks LI), carrying the white flag; Brig. K.S. Torrance, BGS Malaya Command; Lt-Col Ichiji Sugita, Intelligence Officer, 25 Army, IJA; Lt Hishikari, IJA, Interpreter; Brig. T.K. Newbigging, DAG Malaya Command; Lt-Gen. A.E. Percival, GOC Malaya Command, 1941/42. (G.P. Adams Collection)

9. Admiral Lord Louis Mountbatten reading his Order of the Day after the Surrender Ceremony at Singapore, 12 September 1945. On his right: General Sir William Slim and Admiral Sir Arthur Power; on his left: Lt-Gen. R.A. Wheeler and Air Chief Marshal Sir Keith Park. (Broadlands Collection)

10. Col Wild (*right*) and an Australian officer questioning Col Mikizawa at the spot where the executed men of Rimau were buried. Christian crosses over 'Chinese graves'. This picture first appeared in the Illustrated London News, 20 October 1945, in an article headed *No Kid Gloves for Japan*. It is captioned: 'Cruel Commandant of Outram Road Gaol, where he is now held himself, Koshirō Mikizawa shows British officers (one of them an ex-POW) the graves where beheaded victims are buried.'

(Odhams Press Ltd)

11. Cyril Wild in his office at Singapore during war crimes investigations, 1946.

(The Very Revd J. H. S. Wild)

12. Interrogation of Major-General Kojima, GOC Japanese Military Police (*Kempeitai*), Singapore, Malaya, S. Siam and S. Burma – the 'Himmler of Malaya'. The other officer is Lt-Col Haynes, Green Howards, OC War Crimes Investigation Team, N. Malayan Sub. Area.

13. 'In witness box at War Ministry Building, Tokyo, Japan, Col Cyril Hew Dalrymple Wild, British, War Crimes Liaison Officer, testifies for prosecution that Japan violated Siam's neutrality, also to the mistreatment of POW by Japanese, in trial of 27 ex-leaders of Japan.' 11 September 1946.
Photograph by Signal Corps US Army (Wegner)

14. The Very Revd John Wild, Cyril's eldest brother, holding General Yamashita's sword. This was given to Cyril by Admiral Mountbatten after the Japanese surrender. October 1988.

15 & 16. The Union Jack, carried at the fall of Singapore, hidden by Cyril Wild throughout captivity and re-hoisted at the Japanese surrender in 1945. With a dedication beneath it, the flag now hangs in Charterhouse chapel, Cyril's old school. *Photographs by Tim Bradley (OC)*

For security reasons very little was heard, during the war, of that most successful operation, when seven Japanese ships were sunk, totalling 40,000 tons. Since there was no loss of life the whole episode is well documented, but what a different story is that of Lyon's next operation, Rimau, from which there were no survivors.

Operation Rimau, a second attack on enemy shipping in Singapore was, in Lyon's mind, a logical follow-up to his highly successful Jaywick. The Japanese had no knowledge from whence the attack came or by whom it was carried out. Presumably, security around Keppel Harbour and its approaches had been stepped up, but by the time another raid could be mounted this high state of security would probably have slipped back to its old level. Davidson and Page had grave doubts about the wisdom of a second operation, but each was prepared to risk his life again because of his great admiration for and loyalty to Lyon, and the fact that all three knew the waters around Singapore extremely well gave more weight to Lyon's theory.

After months of training at Careening Bay on Garden Island, just south of Fremantle, a party of twenty-three was finally selected, which included three able-seaman from Jaywick. In addition there were five officers, ten NCOs and one private. Sub Lt Riggs, RNVR, of SEAC persuaded Lyon to include him in the party at the last minute.

Apart from physical training, the main emphasis was on Davis submarine escape apparatus, the use of limpets and other explosives, and 'Sleeping Beauties'. These were one-man semi-submersible boats of about twelve feet long, but they proved to be very difficult to master. It seems strange to have preferred the SBs to canoes, which had proved so successful before.

On 11 September 1944 the party left Garden Island in the British mine-laying submarine, *Porpoise*, under the command of Lieutenant-Commander Marchant. They took with them eleven canoes, fifteen Sleeping Beauties and considerable supplies of food, arms and explosives.

They reached Merapas Island, about seventy miles south-east of Singapore, on 23 September and, after a reconnaissance, decided to make Merapas their base. The following day they unloaded a huge supply of stores and Lieutenant Carey volunteered to remain and guard these provisions, as Malays had been seen in the vicinity. *Porpoise* then moved east to Pejantan, in the China Sea, for the next stage of Operation Rimau.

Lyon and Davidson now intended to capture a native craft, from which to launch their final attack. This craft would, of necessity, have to be large enough to carry their Sleeping Beauties and all their stores necessary for the completion of the attack. Luck was on their side when they sighted the junk, *Mustika*, high in the water, having recently discharged her cargo. She appeared to be large enough for their purpose, and so the *Porpoise* surfaced and came alongside. Lyon and Davidson boarded the *Mustika* with five ratings and, at gun point, forced the Malay captain to sail to Pejantan Island, at the same time instructing the boarding party how to handle her under sail.

Loading the SBs into the holds proved a difficult and heavy task and, with the transfer of stores, explosives and ammunition, it took two nights to complete. The Malay crew could not be put ashore, for security reasons, and so the captain and his crew were transferred to the submarine for shipment to Australia. By a strange coincidence the submarine and the junk finally parted on 1 October 1944, exactly one year after the rendezvous with the *Krait*. The *Porpoise* reached Fremantle on 11 October, and handed over the Malay sailors to the authorities. A second British submarine, *Tantalus*, left Fremantle on 15 October to evacuate the Rimau men from Merapas Island on 8 November, with a second rendezvous up to one month later, should the first one fail.

The evacuation submarine was primarily on an offensive patrol from which she was not due to leave until 7 November, and by this date she still had torpedoes and supplies for a further ten days' operations. In view of this, the rendezvous date was put back to 21/22 November, but this was unknown to Lyon and Davidson.

On the evening of 22 November Major Chapman was put ashore on Merapas Island with Corporal Croton. They found no members of the party, but reported that there were signs that they had been there and had, apparently, left in haste. In view of this the submarine returned to Australia.

This is the last official news of Operation Rimau, but now we must return to those three wooden crosses above the 'Chinese' graves.

This, which must rank as one of the most brave and daring operations of the war in the Far-East, would have sunk into oblivion had it not been for Cyril's enquiring mind and his resolute determination to find the answer to such an anomaly. Few people in this country had ever heard of Jaywick or Rimau, but together they are so important historically that it would be remiss of me not to quote Cyril's own verbatim account, entitled *Expedition to Singkep*, which appeared in *Blackwood's Magazine* in October 1946, a month after his untimely death.

He wrote to David:

Do you remember a yarn which I spun about a Far-Eastern commando, the survivors of which died rather well – with a quotation from Sir Alfred Lyall at the end of it? Mr Blackwood is publishing it in his September or October number. I might have made it longer, but it is all fact and no padding.

The numbered and starred footnotes are Cyril's, the footnotes with numbers only are my own.

– – –

BLACKWOOD'S MAGAZINE
N⁰· 1572, OCTOBER 1946, VOL. 260.

EXPEDITION TO SINGKEP
by CYRIL WILD

On 13 February 1942, as the sun set behind the smoke rising from Singapore, SS *Kuala* sailed from Laburnum Steps for Batavia. Her passengers were mainly nursing-sisters, with a party of Public Works Dept men, some RAF technicians, and a few civilians. They had suffered some casualties from bombing while waiting to embark, and were bombed again without effect before they sailed. At dawn on 14 February the *Kuala* anchored off Pompong Island in the Rhio Archipelago, 300 yards from SS *Tien Kuang*, which had left Singapore in company with her. A mile away lay SS *Kung Wo*, with a decided list from bombing received the night before. Boats were lowered to fetch foliage from the shore for camouflage, and two were still away when a flight of Japanese bombers came over at 11.30 to finish off the *Kung Wo*. They sank her in a few minutes. The *Kuala*'s turn came next: the first stick set her afire, and two more followed. Women and wounded were sent away in the remaining boats, and the rest of the ship's company, including some of the women, took to the water, supporting themselves on mattresses and spars. Unfortunately the current carried them down towards the *Tien Kuang*, to which the bombers were now turning their attention. Four sticks were dropped, which did little apparent damage to the ship, but killed and wounded a number of people in the water. The last flight of bombers dropped their load on shore, causing further casualties among those who had already landed. The survivors of the three ships divided into two parties of about 400 and 250 and made their way to the north and south of the island, which was about a mile across, covered with dense jungle and uninhabited. Their intention was to avoid the unhealthy neighbourhood of the ships, should the bombers return; for although the *Kuala* was now ablaze, the *Tien Kuang* still offered a tempting target. The ship's whaler was used at night to maintain contact between the two camps and to carry water from a small spring at the north of the island to the people in the south. After dark a party of volunteers boarded the *Tien Kuang* and obtained a quantity of stores and medical supplies. An attempt was made to raise steam, but the sea had risen too high in her engine-room. She was therefore scuttled by opening a sea-cock, before she could attract more bombers.

On the afternoon of 16 February a small sampan arrived, manned by three Malays, who said that on all the small neighbouring islands there were more survivors of ships sunk by bombing. They were asked to obtain food and assistance, and set off again, promising to do their best. At 1 a.m. the following morning they returned with small supplies of coconuts and rice. The owner of the sampan, Ali by name, urged that an attempt should be made to reach the island of Senajang, where help could be obtained. Mr I. G. Salmond, who spoke both Dutch and Malay, was chosen for this task, and set off in the sampan, taking with him eight wounded RAF men and one Sepoy. They left Pompong with the Malays about 1.30 a.m. One of the wounded died a few hours later, but the craft was so small that it was impossible to dispose of the body without capsizing. It was therefore kept on board until they could bury it on Senajang, where they arrived about 3 p.m. on 17 February.

Here Salmond hastened to meet the Amir, Silalahi, a Malay chieftain, with authority over a hundred islands in the Archipelago. His title in Dutch is '*Hoofd der Onderafdeeling Blakang Daik*'.

On hearing the story of Pompong, the Amir at once pledged all the help of himself and his people to the hundreds of British thus stranded in his territory. He himself set off for the island of Redjai to collect motor *tongkans*, and undertook to send the news by the first of these to the nearest Dutch Controlleur, at Dabot, on Singkep Island. During the next two weeks the Amir worked unceasingly day and night, scouring the islands of the Archipelago with a fleet of *tongkans* and sampans to collect survivors, and stinting his own people of food and shelter in his determination to succour these sufferers of an alien race. He did this out of his great humanity, without thought of favour or reward, knowing full well the danger of reprisals from the Japanese, whose arrival was expected daily.

By the end of February nearly one thousand British men, women, and children had been ferried over to the mouth of the Indragiri River, fifty or sixty miles away, most of them in native craft, but some in small ships of the Royal Navy, such as H M S *Hung Jau*. From the Indragiri River they crossed Sumatra to Padang, where most of them were evacuated by the Royal Navy. Many hundreds in England and Australia today owe their liberty and lives to the Amir Silalahi.

Mr Salmond remained in charge on Senajang and Singkep Islands until the last of the survivors had passed through. On leaving Singkep he took the Amir by the hand and said, 'I promise that when the day comes I shall return from Singapore with the British Navy to drive out the Japanese.' 'No, Tuan,' replied the Amir quietly, 'I shall come to Singapore to meet you, and we shall return together with the British Navy to liberate my people.'

Mr Salmond reached Padang on 10 March, some days after the last British ship had left. There he met a man of the same temper as himself in Lieut-Colonel F. J. Dillon, M C, who had been ordered to leave Singapore for India on 13 February. Dillon, too, had risked his own chance of escape by staying for a month in central Sumatra until he had organised transport to the west coast for the many hundreds who had escaped from Singapore. Mr Salmond joined him as interpreter, and with a party of eight officers they left Sumatra in a small sailing junk on 16 March and set their course for Ceylon. When dawn broke on 4 April they were well on their way with a favouring wind, and thought that their worst danger, from the daily reconnaissance of land-based aircraft, was behind them. Instead, out of the mist emerged three Japanese naval tankers; and forty-eight hours later they were all back in Singapore, as prisoners.

August 1945 found Dillon in Changi Camp, near Singapore, after our sojourn together on the Burma-Siam Railway with F Force. (I can only hope that the gratitude of the surviving British and Australian members of that party, which lost 3,100 out of 7,000 up by the Three Pagodas Pass in seven months, goes some way to console him for the unlucky chance which overtook him in mid-ocean.) The officer who relieved us was Lieut-Colonel Bob Stewart of the Canadian Army, formerly of the Vancouver Police. He had parachuted some weeks before into Johore from India to join the Chinese guerrillas. One day he arrived in Changi Camp in a Chevrolet roadster, commandeered from a Japanese general in Johore Bahru. (Even the Japanese were startled at the contrast between his magnificent physique and our somewhat attenuated frames.) With Stewart I spent a happy week touring the island, with a Union Jack flying on the roadster. We visited the Civilian Internment Camp at Sime Road, and all the camps of the loyal Indian prisoners-of-war.

Later, Major Cooper, an aerodrome engineer, arrived from the Cocos Islands in a Mosquito. With him, as his interpreter, I visited all the aerodromes on the island, to measure them up and see that the Japs had taken the propellers off their planes. While General Itagaki still kept up his boasting that he would fight for Malaya and Singapore, we saw his men piling their arms and shuffling northwards across the Causeway in their thousands.

So far the local population had dared do no more than give surreptitious V-for-victory and thumbs-up signs as our car with the Union Jack sped past. But today, as we returned from Tengah Aerodrome, we could scarcely drive through the cheering crowds in Singapore. (Cyril describes the incident when they were instructed by Major-General Mansergh to take the Union Jack off their car. See page 70).

Next day I joined the unit which had been diverted to War Crimes. Our first task was to discover the fate of certain missing pilots. A well-meant tip from a Malay driver took us on the day after the landing to Outram Road Gaol to interrogate Mikizawa, our first prisoner. Mikizawa, as commandant of the civil side of the prison, had a good deal on his conscience, having lost 1,200 Asiatic prisoners from starvation during the last fourteen months of the war. It was not long, therefore, before he led us to a lonely stretch of country near Reformatory Road, where his driver had taken him to an execution in July. He prodded about among the scrub until he found three newly made mounds with wooden crosses on them. This, he thought, was the place. The heath around was pitted with half-filled depressions and open graves, among stunted bushes and the insect-eating plant call Dutchman's pipe. Evidently it was a favourite execution-ground of the Japanese. Why, then, were these the only graves marked with crosses? Mikizawa did not know: they were Chinese whom he had seen executed. Unfortunately the authorities did not permit us to exhume, and the matter remained a mystery.

A week or so later the Amir Silalahi, long since deposed by the Japanese, arrived in Singapore, having escaped from Singkep Island in a *tongkan*. He asked for and met Mr Salmond, who had just been released from the Sime Road Internment Camp. Salmond brought him to us – a young Malay, with finely cut aquiline features, and the sad but dignified air of an exiled chieftain, conscious of his integrity and worth. He had two stories to tell. The first was that a well-armed Japanese garrison, with its headquarters on Singkep Island, was still terrorising the Lingga Archipelago. Among them were twenty-seven members of the Japanese Gestapo, the *Kempeitai*, of whom twelve (he gave us their names) had been heavily involved in the Double Tenth case, so called because it was on 10 October 1943 that more than forty of the British internees in Singapore had been arrested by the *Kempeitai*. Fifteen of them later died from torture and ill-treatment at their hands. His second story was that in December 1944 ten British and Australians, members of a raiding party, had been captured in the Lingga Archipelago and had been kept as prisoners on Singkep Island until they were taken to Singapore.

The task of reoccupying Malaya was such that it was not until October that we could take action. Meantime, the Amir stayed on patiently in Singapore. We took him to the Great World Amusement Park, and to the Cathay to see 'Tunisian Victory'. He was an appreciative and forbearing guest, but at the end of each evening he would ask us, 'When will the British Navy be coming to liberate my people?'

At last, one morning in October, four MLs set forth from Collyer Quay. On board, besides our excellent Naval hosts, were half a platoon of paratroops under a subaltern; Major Sheppard of the Malayan Civil Service, who had planned the expedition and had himself twice experienced *Kempeitai* methods of interrogation in captivity; another ex-internee, Mr Leonard Knight of the Police, engaged like Sheppard on the Double Tenth investigation; a Dutch official; myself, and Mr Salmond and the Amir Silalahi, together keeping their engagement of three and a half years before. Next morning the Amir was gazing proudly from the deck at the palm-fringed beaches of Singkep Island and the jungle-clad peaks beyond. On the pier waited the Japanese garrison-commander, who had been warned by wireless of our coming. We split into four parties: Sheppard went into the little town of Dabot with Salmond and the Amir to assist the new Dutch Controlleur to take over; Knight set off to organise and arm the police; another officer with a Malay interpreter inquired into the Amir's story of the missing British and Australian party, while I went up the hill behind the town to the *Kempeitai* headquarters. On calling the roll[1] I found that one badly wanted man was missing, Miyazaki, a Jap-Malay half-caste, who had interpreted for the *Kempeitai* in the Double Tenth, particularly during the torture of the Bishop of Singapore. On the principle of setting a thief to catch a thief, I selected the four toughest-looking *kempei* and sent them off in two flying-squads to find him. Long before my time-limit of one hour was up, two of the *kempei* had brought him back well roped between them, having found him in a small sailing-boat, struggling to catch a breeze that would take him to one of the neighbouring islands.[2]

We left for Singapore again that night, with twenty-five Japanese squatting in the bows of our four M Ls. Also among our captives, at the Controlleur's request, was the Malay quisling who had usurped the Amir's place. The Amir himself stood waving farewell to us from the end of Singkep's pier until he and then his island were lost to our view in the gathering darkness.

Among our trophies was the admission book of the local police station and a scrap of paper bearing the names of a British officer, a warrant officer, and an able seaman, each pencilled in block letters in a different hand. The admission book, kept in Malay, showed that on 18 and 19 December six 'white men' had been admitted, and all had been transferred to Singapore on 23 December. A later entry showed that three more 'white men' had been admitted on 28 – 29 December and had left for Singapore on 8 January 1945. The charge against each was the same, 'enemy of the State'. Attempts had been made to write the names of some of them, but, apart from those on the scrap of paper, only one was clear – 'R. M. Ingleton, Major, Royal Marines. British.' Two others were marked 'Australian', and one 'Australian (British)'.

These were the only clues when we took up the hunt for the nine 'white men' in Singapore. There was no trace of such people having ever been in a prisoner-of-war camp, and the Japanese were in a conspiracy to tell us nothing. No single survivor, as it turned out, remained to tell the tale, and no written record of theirs remained beyond that found on Singkep. Yet within a month we knew their story in full, and how and where each one of them (not only these nine, but fourteen of their comrades) had met his end. Moreover, only one of the Japanese concerned had escaped the net, and he by suicide at the surrender. Here, then, is the story.

On 11 September 1944, HM Submarine *Porpoise* left Perth, W. Australia, with a strange party of twenty-three on board, in addition to her normal crew. The Royal Navy, the Royal Marines, and the Army had each provided their quota; seven were officers, and the proportion of Australians to British was about two to one. The leader was Lieut-Colonel I. Lyon of the Gordon Highlanders, who had won his DSO for a brilliant achievement in 1943, when a party led by him blew up six Japanese ships in Singapore Roads and returned safely to Australia. The object of the present expedition was to repeat that exploit. At Merapas Island they left the submarine, and arranged a rendezvous with her there for 6 November.[3] After forming their base on shore they embarked in a captured junk for Singapore. By 6 October they had reached Puloe Samboe, just outside the harbour. They were awaiting their moment to strike when a police launch approached their junk and forced them to open fire. As surprise was essential to their operation, Lyon was forced to abandon it for the time being. He therefore gave orders to withdraw independently to Merapas in four small parties in rubber boats. The Japanese encountered Lyon's own party on Sole Island. In the night action which followed, Lyon and one other officer[4] were killed, after killing the Japanese commander and killing and wounding several more. The remainder reached Merapas Island safely, and joined forces with the other three parties who had likewise suffered some casualties. The Japanese discovered them on 4 November, four days before the submarine was due to arrive. In the action which followed, the Japanese were at first repulsed with heavy loss, but our people were later compelled to leave Merapas and continue their withdrawal to the south. The fighting went on from island to island, until twelve had been killed or died, and ten had been taken prisoner. Of these an able seaman died shortly after capture. The other nine were lodged in Singkep Police Station, and were then taken to Singapore. One more, an officer, was captured later when his rubber boat stranded on some fishing-stakes not far from Timor. Of his two companions in this fantastic voyage one had been killed by natives and the other taken by a shark. He, too, was brought to Singapore and lodged with the other nine in the Water Police Station, from which they were transferred in February to Outram Road Gaol. Of their life in captivity we have a remarkably full record. It is clear that from the first they were regarded with respect, verging on awe, by the Japanese, and in consequence were exceptionally well treated. A well-disposed Japanese interpreter[5] supplied them regularly with books, chocolates, and cigarettes. The officers had little doubt what their fate was likely to be, but the whole party remained in excellent spirits and good health until the end. They were sentenced to death by a military court on 5 July 1945, and on the 7th they were beheaded in the execution-ground off Reformatory Road. Their graves were those which we discovered by chance just two months after. In an unmarked grave close by were buried the Chinese victims of the later execution witnessed by Mikizawa.

Let the Japanese themselves tell the last chapter. The first paragraph is from the closing address of the prosecuting officer:[6]

'With such fine determination they infiltrated into the Japanese area. We do not hesitate to call them the real heroes of a forlorn hope. It has been fortunate for us that their intention was frustrated half-way, but when we fathom their intention and share their feelings we cannot but spare a tear for them. The valorous spirit of these men reminds us of the daring enterprise of our heroes of the Naval Special Attack Corps who died in May 1942 in their attack on Sydney Harbour. The same admiration and respect that the Australian Government, headed by the Premier and all the Australian people, showed to those heroes of ours we must return to these heroes in our presence. When the deed is so heroic, its sublime spirit must be respected, and its success or failure becomes a secondary matter. These heroes must have left Australia with sublime patriotism flaming in their breasts, and with the confident expectation of all the Australian people on their shoulders. The last moment of a hero must be historic and it must be dramatic. Heroes have more regard for their reputation than for anything else. As we respect them, so we feel our duty of glorifying their last moments as they deserve: and by our doing so the names of these heroes will remain in the heart of the British and Australian people for evermore. In these circumstances, I consider that a death sentence should be given to each of the accused'.

Major Ingleton thanked the court for referring to them as 'patriotic heroes'.[1]

'After the trial all the members of the party were given extra rations, and, in accordance with their request, were kept together in one room so that they could freely converse with one another. The attitude was really admirable. They were always clear and bright,and not a single shadow of dismal or melancholy mood did they show. All who saw them were profoundly impressed'.[2]

'They all knew they were going to be executed. When they left their prison to enter the two trucks in which their executioners were waiting, they were in high spirits, laughing and talking and shaking hands with one another. All of us prisoners were amazed'.[3]

On arrival at the execution-ground at 10 a.m. on 7 July, 'they were all given cigarettes and rested. Then, in accordance with their request, they were allowed to shake hands with one another. They all stood up, shook hands merrily and even laughingly in a very harmonious manner, and bade each other farewell. The sky was clear and the scenery was beautiful'.[4]

'Major Ingleton, on behalf of the whole party, requested the commandant of the prison and the prosecuting officer to tell the Japanese interpreter that they were all most grateful for the courtesy and kindness which he had shown them for a long time past. He said again that they must not forget to give the interpreter this message. All who heard him were deeply moved'.*5

'The execution started and it was over by noon. Every member of the party went to his death calmly and composedly, and there was not a single person there who was not inspired by their fine attitude'.*6

'Major-General Ohtsuka reported to the 7th Area Army Commander and the Chief of Staff on the completion of this execution and commented on the sublime and glorious manner in which these men had met their death'.*7

At a Staff Conference of the 7th Area Army, 'Major-General Ohtsuka reported on the patriotism, fearless enterprise, heroic behaviour, and sublime end of all members of this party, praising them as the flower of chivalry, which should be taken as a model by the Japanese. He concluded by saying that all Japanese soldiers should be inspired by their fine attitude, and on reflection must feel the necessity of bracing up their own spirits in emulation, if they hoped to win the war'.*8

Three weeks later Japan surrendered. There is evidence that the Japanese were anxious to avoid the death sentence. It was in fact suggested to the prisoners before their trial that they should adopt a humble attitude and plead for mercy. Instead, down to the last corporal and able seaman they remained resolute and defiant to the last. A young Australian captain,*9 who had accompanied Lyon on his earlier expedition also, was asked by the court, 'Did you yourself kill any Japanese soldiers?' He replied in clear and deliberate tones, 'I am an officer in the British army, and I know that my aim was good.' Not one of them can have dreamt that a single word of his conduct or his fate would ever be heard in England or Australia. What, then, was the secret of their cheerful endurance in captivity and of the light-hearted courage with which they met their end?

> Why? Am I bidding for glory's roll?
> I shall be murdered and clean forgot.
> Is it a bargain to save my soul?
> God, whom I trust in, bargains not.
> Yet, for the honour of England's race,
> Can I not live and accept disgrace?

I must be gone to the crowd untold
Of men, by the cause that they served, unknown,
Who moulder in myriad graves of old.
Never a story and never a stone
Tells of the fellows who died like me,
Just for the sake of the Old Countree.[7]

It has been my privilege, little by little, to piece together their story, and to mark their graves with this stone.

CYRIL WILD

NOTES

[1] 30 of them.

[2] Cyril wrote later of an incident that occurred at this point: 'Just before embarking I addressed the *Kempeitai* Captain in front of his own men. A considerable crowd of Malay islanders, and some of the paratroops and ML crews were there too. I had got through about half what I had to say when the fellow fainted! So much for a man who had tortured and murdered his way through the Japanese occupation in Malaya and Singapore and been for the last 18 months the tyrant of the Rhio and Lingga Archipelagos!'

[3] Cyril made an error here. The rendezvous date was the night of 8/9 November, as mentioned earlier in this chapter.

[4] Lieutenant H.R. Ross, British Army.

[5] Hiroyuki Furuta, who was the interpreter at my own court-martial.

[6] Major Haruo Kamiya, who was one of the three judges at my own court-martial.

[7] Poem by Sir Alfred Lyall.

[*1] Translation of proceedings of Military Court.

[*2] Translation of Records of Judiciary Department, 7th Area Army.

[*3] Interrogation of Korean witness.

[*4] Translation of Records of Judiciary Department, 7th Area Army.

[*5] Interrogation of Japanese witness.

[*6] Translation of Records of Judiciary Department, 7th Area Army.

[*7] Translation of Records of Judiciary Department, 7th Area Army.

[*8] Translation of Records of Judiciary Department, 7th Area Army.

[*9] Capt. R.C. Page, DSO.

Chapter 7
YAMASHITA

In September and October 1945 Cyril was working in Singapore and Malaya with E Group on War Crimes Investigations, under the auspices of Admiral Lord Mountbatten, Supreme Allied Commander, South-East Asia. He gradually built up a dossier on all Japanese believed to be responsible for crimes against Allied servicemen, and civilians of many nationalities, but inevitably there were gaps and missing links as time had been so short, owing to the rapid repatriation of so many possible witnesses.

Cyril felt that he might be able to fill in some of these gaps if given the chance to have a face-to-face talk with Lt-Gen. Tomoyuki Yamashita. 'The Tiger of Malaya' had been the High Commander of the Nippon 25th Army in Malaya during hostilities and immediately afterwards. He had proved himself to be such an able soldier and tactition that General Tōjō exiled him to Manchuria for two years, as he saw in him a potential rival to himself. However, he was later brought back to command the Japanese 14th Army, where he held out in the Madre Sierra mountains of the Philippines until the end of the war. He was in Manila awaiting trial when Cyril made his request for a confrontation with him. If Yamashita disclaimed any knowledge of certain atrocities, he might be willing to incriminate other formation commanders under his command.

The Commanding General of Army Forces Western Pacific agreed to a request from the Supreme Allied Commander South-East Asia that one of his own officers could interview General Yamashita prior to his trial and, as a result of this, a telegram was sent from Admiral Lord Mountbatten's headquarters on 20 October 1945, with a copy to South-East Asia Command HQ, E Group.

CITE 457/A Confidential / OPTNL PRIORITY

For 14th Army

1. CG AFWESPAC has agreed that an officer proceed to Manila from SEAC to interrogate General Yamashita regarding the atrocities committed in Malaya. Yamashita now being tried in Manila and interrogation must

therefore take place at such a time and in such manner as would not interfere with this trial.

2. Officer should arrive in Manila as soon as possible.

3. ALFSEA[1] and HQ E Group have agreed that Major Wild now working with E Group in Singapore should carry out interrogation.

4. Request you arrange Wild proceeds to Manila earliest to report to the HQ of General Styer the CG AFWESPAC.

5. Understand Wild is recovered POW and will therefore not be sent unless willing and fit to proceed.

FOR CG AFWESPAC

6. Wild is fluent Japanese speaker and has special knowledge of case and Yamashita but is not legally trained officer. Very grateful therefore if you would arrange to give him any legal assistance that may be necessary.

On 23 October Cyril flew to Manila and reported to Lieutenant-General W.D. Styer at the HQ of United States Army Forces Western Pacific, where he was handed this introductory note to pass on to the Defence Counsel, War Crimes Commission:

Headquarters
United States Army Forces Western Pacific
Office of the Commanding General

Subject: Interview with General Yamashita by Major C.H.D. Wild

This will introduce Major C.H.D. Wild of Admiral Mountbatten's Command who is in Manila to assist in the trial of General Yamashita. Major Wild is particularly desirous of interviewing General Yamashita prior to the trial in order that he may obtain information concerning General Yamashita's activities in Malaya, which might otherwise not be brought out in the course of the trial.

If you have no objection, I should appreciate your giving Major Wild whatever assistance you feel is warranted.

signed: J. T. Jackson
Major, Ord. Dept Executive

Cyril's report on the proceedings of his interview with Yamashita is self-explanatory:

REPORT ON INTERROGATION OF
GENERAL TOMOYUKI YAMASHITA
BY MAJOR C.H.D. WILD, 'E' GROUP, SEAC
AT MANILA, 28 OCTOBER 1945

1. In compliance with SACSEA's 457/A dated 20 October 1945 to Commanding General, AF WES PAC, I left Singapore on 23 October via Labuan and Morotai, and reported on 27 October to Lt-Gen. W.D.

Styer's HQ at Manila. I was referred by them to Colonel A.C. Carpenter and Lt-Colonel K.C. Schwartz, Chief and Executive Officer respectively of the War Crimes Branch, from whom I received every facility and assistance. As a result of this, I was enabled to interrogate General Yamashita on the morning of 28 October 1945. His trial opened on 29 October, and interrogation during or subsequent to this would, in my opinion, have had little chance of success.

2. A list of all known atrocities against British and Imperial Forces with which Yamashita could be connected is attached.[2] These consist of atrocities committed in Malaya during and shortly after action, i.e. before and after 15 February 1942. Reference numbers are shown against those cases concerning which I interrogated.

3. I had been forewarned that Yamashita was unlikely to talk, as he had resisted previous interrogations, denying all knowledge of atrocities. I started, therefore, by reminding him of our previous meeting at the British surrender at Bukit Timah, Singapore. We then discussed the Malayan Campaign, and he expressed his admiration for the generalship of Lt-General Sir Lewis Heath, Comdg III Indian Corps, and enquired after him and Lady Heath. I then referred to the terms of his letter to Lt-General A.E. Percival, GOC Malaya, requesting the surrender of Singapore. This he remembered having had dropped from the air on 10 February 1942. He said, 'That letter was entirely sincere. Your troops in Malaya did fight extremely bravely.' I said that on several occasions in captivity I had found his letter a useful document to quote when I was told by Japanese officers that owing to the unconditional nature of the surrender of Singapore we had forfeited all rights as prisoners-of-war.

He said, 'Not officers, surely: you mean private soldiers.' I repeated, 'Officers', and he expressed his disapproval. I then said that immediately after the capitulation we had regarded ourselves as prisoners of an enemy who had fought fairly and from whom fair treatment could be expected. In both respects we had been quickly disillusioned: in particular we had soon heard from surviving witnesses of a number of atrocities perpetrated by the Japanese during or just after action. Yamashita expressed his past ignorance and present disapproval of such things, and in proof of the latter he agreed to assist by naming those responsible.

4. He also disclaimed all previous knowledge of each of these atrocities, as I recounted them in detail. He took notes, including the names of some witnesses. He did not question any of the evidence. On several occasions he condemned the perpetrators in fairly strong terms.

5. *Ref. No. 1.* (Two massacres of Australian and Indian wounded and prisoners after the battle of Muar.) Yamashita stated that the 5th Division under Lt-General Takurō Matsui was attacking down the central Johore road. The outflanking movement on the right, including the landings near Muar, was performed by the Konoye Division ('a very good Division'). This Division fought the battle of Muar and conducted the pursuit. He

agreed that troops of this Division must be considered responsible for both massacres. The Division Commander was Lt-General Takuma Nishimura, now in Japan. Yamashita agreed that Nishimura should be interrogated and wrote out his name in Japanese characters.

6. *Ref. No. 2.* (Presumed shooting of L/Sgt Keiller, AIF) Concerning this case, I asked only what troops were operating around Yong Peng on 22 January 1942. The answer was that they were more likely to have been men of the Konoye Division (Lt-Gen. Nishimura) than of the 5th Division (Lt-Gen. Matsui).

7. *Ref. No. 3.* (Alexandra Hospital Massacre.) Yamashita said, 'I never heard of this until today.' He spoke strongly of 'the fools who had done this senseless, brutal thing'. He stated that in the assault on Singapore, the Konoye Division was on the left, immediately west of the Causeway: the 5th Division was in the centre: and the 18th Division (Lt-General Renya Mutaguchi) was on the right. The 18th Division made the initial crossing and continued to form the right (i.e. western) wing until the fall of Singapore. He said that troops of the 18th Division must have been responsible for the massacre and that Lt-General Mutaguchi (now in Japan) should be interrogated.

8. *Ref. No. 4.* (Shooting of 14 Australian prisoners, 19 February 1942.) Yamashita agreed that the shooting of these prisoners contravened the capitulation of 15 February. He expressed his disapproval and said with some emphasis that if he had known of this incident at the time, he would 'of course' have punished those responsible. He said that Pasir Panjang was in the area of the 18th Division, but that the troops there on 19 February might have been a Transport Unit following up the 18th Division as it moved in closer to Singapore after the capitulation. He said that in either case, Lt-General Mutaguchi should be interrogated in order to ascertain the Japanese responsible. He suggested that Japanese soldiers might have been ordered to transfer the prisoners to Changi POW Camp and might have taken it on themselves to shoot them on the way. I referred him to McCann's report, which clearly states that the men had their hands tied behind their backs while still at Pasir Panjang and that the escort and firing party were commanded by a Japanese officer.

9. *Ref. No. 5.* (Massacre of Chinese in Singapore.) Yamashita said that after the fall of Singapore the three Divisions were kept outside the city and none of them were allowed to enter it. He drew a map to illustrate their positions. The Divisions, therefore, could not be held responsible. Maintenance of order in the city was the responsibility of the *Kempeitai*, who were entitled to kill bad characters, such as robbers and those in possession of weapons. I said that many hundreds, even thousands, of innocent civilians had been among those killed, and that the 'crime' of most of them was solely that they were young and Chinese. Yamashita said, 'Innocent? It should have been only the robbers and those with arms.' I asked who gave the orders to kill these people. He replied that the *Kempeitai* did not need any orders but had full discretion and powers.

Interrogator: 'Was the commander of the *Kempeitai* in Singapore in February 1942 then solely responsible for killing these civilians?'

Yamashita: 'Yes. He was responsible.'

Interrogator: 'What was his name and that of the senior military officer responsible for the city?'

Yamashita: 'I do not now remember!'[3]

Interrogator: 'Were you informed of these killings?'

Yamashita: 'No. I was not informed.'

Interrogator: 'Was that because you were too senior an officer to be troubled with such trifling matters?'

Yamashita: 'That is correct.'

Interrogator: 'How long did you stay in Singapore after the capitulation of 15 February 1942?'

Yamashita: 'Until June.'

10. I did not refer to the other two cases, as one occurred during action and the other was obviously a piece of independent barbarity against an isolated victim.[4] Yamashita would certainly have disclaimed knowledge of either (probably correctly), and both are lacking in details of location. Also my time was limited by the claims of the Defence Counsel for the forthcoming trial, by whose courtesy this interrogation was made possible.

11. In conclusion, I asked General Yamashita if he had any special statement to make which I could pass on to the Supreme Allied Commander South-East Asia. He replied, 'No, nothing special': then added, 'Until today I had truly never heard of any of these matters. Please tell Admiral Mountbatten that. Tell him, too, that on learning that Japanese soldiers did these things I have been astounded.'

signed: C.H.D. Wild
MAJOR, E Group, SEAC
MANILA, 29 October 1945

The following is a covering letter that Cyril sent to the Supreme Allied Commander South-East Asia, with his personal report on his meeting with General Yamashita, with a copy to 14th Army:

INTERROGATION OF GENERAL TOMOYUKI YAMASHITA
AT MANILA

Reference your 457/A dated 20 October 1945 to CG AFWESPAC.

1. The report of my interrogation of General Yamashita at Manila on 28 October 1945 is attached. Copies of this were handed by me to Col Carpenter, Chief of War Crimes Branch, Manila, and to Lt-Col Dunne,

Senior War Crimes Officer, Adv. HQ Aust. Milit. Forces, Morotai. I informed Lt-Col Dunne that action on this report would be taken by SACSEA only. He marked his copy accordingly.

2. Neither Army Forces Western Pacific nor the War Crimes Branch were prepared to do more than *recommend* to Yamashita's Defence Counsel, a group of American Legal Officers under a Colonel, that they should grant me an interview with Yamashita, 'if they had no objection'. In fact they did object, and it was only after some argument that I obtained an interview, limited to one hour, in private.

3. Yamashita gave the impression of speaking the truth when he disclaimed previous knowledge of these Malayan atrocities. It is of course possible that an officer of his rank in the Japanese army would be told nothing of the behaviour of his troops towards prisoners and civilians and would consider it beneath his dignity to enquire. It is expected that the defence at his trial in Manila will largely be based on this contention, while one of the objects of the prosecution is to establish the precedent that a commander's plea of ignorance does not absolve him of responsibility for atrocities committed by forces under his command.

4. Interrogation of Lieutenant-Generals Nishimura and Mutaguchi in Japan should disclose the subordinate units and commanders more immediately responsible. The threat of putting the pair of them on trial as war-criminals will probably be enough to make them talk. Also the news that Yamashita has himself nominated them for interrogation and has condemned these acts will be a further strong inducement. It is, in any case, a notable and helpful feature of interrogation of the Japanese since the surrender that senior officers are generally willing to give away their subordinates, while junior officers and other ranks are ready to incriminate their seniors. This abject reversal of the long tradition of personal loyalty is one of the most striking proofs of their awareness of defeat.

5. Some suggestions concerning the further interrogations which will be necessary in Japan are attached.[7]

6. Yamashita showed such interest in discussing the Malayan Campaign that I asked the War Crimes Branch for a further interview at which I would have dealt with this subject only. I could undoubtedly have obtained from him much information of value to the military historian. I also counted on getting a written directive from him to Lieutenant-Generals Nishimura and Mutaguchi, instructing them to assist in the investigation of these crimes. Unfortunately the Defence Counsel would not agree to any interrogation during the trial, which started next day and is likely to last a month.

7. The delay in forwarding this report is regretted. It was caused by lack of air-transport from Morotai and Labuan on the return journey.

8. An Analysis of the organisation of the Americans' War Crimes Branches in Tokyo and Manila will be forwarded separately. Upwards of a thousand personnel are employed at their two Branches, including 14 Colonels, 29

Lt-Colonels and 155 Majors, with a high proportion of legal officers among them.

signed: C.H.D. Wild
MAJOR
OC 'E' Group South
8 November 1945

As a result of Cyril's interview with Yamashita he was able to prepare notes for the interrogations of Generals Nishimura, Mutaguchi, Fukuye and Arimura. In these notes, which conclude this chapter, he explained fully the events surrounding the massacres at Parit Sulong. The 'Selerang Incident' and the ill-treatment of prisoners-of-war on the Burma-Siam railway have already been described in Chapter 4, but the massacre at Alexandra Hospital needs further expansion by an analysis of Cyril's evidence at the Major War Crimes Tribunal in Tokyo, based on a report by Major Bull, and confirmed by the commandant of the hospital, Colonel Craven.

On 12 February the Allied front line was withdrawn in the rear of Alexandra Hospital, and Colonel Craven was notified of this by Malaya Command HQ. This, the largest military hospital in Singapore or Malaya, was already well marked with Red Cross signs, but in anticipation of an unopposed arrival of Japanese forces, extra Red Cross flags were displayed at every approach.

On 14 February the Japanese stormed into the hospital and bayonetted or shot everyone on the ground floor, killing a wounded soldier on the operating table, and the surgeon. The anaesthetist survived his bayonet wounds and subsequently told Cyril of the nightmare ordeal, showing him the scars on his body and hands.

Major Bull stood on the top veranda of the hospital, holding a Red Cross flag at full stretch of his arms, but a bullet passed through the flag, striking the wall behind him. He could see a Japanese officer below him directing the fire.

Meanwhile, Japanese soldiers were going through the whole hospital, clearing from the wards all patients who could stand and driving them out of the building. Captain Allardyce, a medical officer friend of Cyril's from Kōbe, volunteered to find a senior Japanese officer and try to stop what was happening, as he himself spoke Japanese. But he was taken with the 200 wounded and medical staff to houses about half a mile away, where they were crowded into small rooms, with doors and windows shut, for the night. Five died of suffocation and, next taken out and bayonetted or machine-gunned. Captain Allardyce was among those killed, but five managed to survive the ordeal.

In addition to the 200 wounded personnel who were killed, 20 British medical officers and 60 medical orderlies died at the hands of the merciless Japanese. Cyril's men from River Valley Road Camp collected and buried their bodies three months later.

NOTES ON PROPOSED INTERROGATION OF
JAPANESE GENERAL OFFICERS IN JAPAN

Refer to para. 4 of E Group (South)'s letter of 8 November 1945 regarding interrogation of General Yamashita.

1. (i) *Lieutenant-General Takuma Nishimura, GOC Konoye Division at battle of Muar, January 1942.*

There is good reason to suppose that the Parit Sulong massacre of 110 Australian and 35/40 Indian wounded, by machine-gunning and burning alive with petrol on 22 January 1942, was personally ordered by Lt-Gen. Nishimura. The sole surviving witness is Lt B. Hackney, 2/29 Bn, AIF, whose evidence has recently been confirmed by discovery of the victims' remains. The following information was given to me verbally by Hackney shortly before the Japanese surrender. It is also contained in a lengthy written report which he took back to Australia, but is omitted from the short synopsis of which SACSEA hold a copy.

(a) These surviving wounded, from an ambulance-column which the Australians had been trying to extricate for three days, were confined on capture in two small rooms of a block of coolie-quarters adjacent to the Muar-Parit Sulong road. Along this road troops in M T, tanks and artillery of the Konoye Division were pouring past for many hours in pursuit.

(b) Then a special convoy halted on the road. It consisted of two groups of medium tanks, in front and rear, with a number of staff-cars between them. From these a very senior officer and his staff emerged, and were paid full compliments by the troops on the spot.

(c) This officer inspected the wounded from the doorway. They were in great distress, lying piled on one another's bodies on the floor. Many of them had fresh wounds, in addition to those which they had received three days or more before. They had been refused water by the Japanese, who had amused themselves by bringing it to them and pouring it on the ground outside.

(d) After his inspection, this officer was seen to give orders to the Japanese outside before reentering his staff-car. Full compliments were again paid him and the convoy moved off.

(e) The remaining Japanese immediately proceeded with the preparations for the massacre. The prisoners were fastened into small groups with ropes

100

and signal-wire. There was not enough of this, and Hackney and a few others were not so fastened, but their hands were trussed up behind their backs. On being moved off at the point of the bayonet, Hackney's broken leg gave way and he was left where he fell. He continued to sham dead, although he was clubbed and bayonetted several times on the ground. He still bears the scars on his head and body.

(f) After the firing had stopped, a number of Japanese walked past him to the road and returned carrying tins of petrol. The cries and screams broke out afresh and shortly ceased.

(g) Hackney was joined that night by Sgt Croft, 2/29 Bn, and one other Australian. These two had rolled away from the pile of bodies before it was set alight. Their clothing still reeked of petrol. Neither of them survived.

(h) The Konoye Division was the only formation in the Parit Sulong area. It is highly probable that only the Divisional Commander would have travelled in such a strongly protected convoy. Lieutenant Hackney, an intelligent and reliable witness, might still be able to identify a full-length photograph of Lt-General Nishimura, in uniform and cap.

(i) In August or September 1942 a party of British prisoners were taken to the Muar area from Kuala Lumpur gaol to take part in a film of the battle. A British officer, who had heard Hackney's story in the gaol, asked a Japanese officer why they had killed our wounded. The answer was that a Regimental Commander (Colonel) had been killed in action and that the troops were told to take no prisoners, in revenge.

(j) Regarding the separate executions by beheading of 200 Australians and Indians, the only evidence consists of the statements of two surviving Sepoys and some local natives, and the discovery of the victims' skulls and bones.

1. (ii) It is suggested that the interrogating officer, after referring to Yamashita's statement, should assume as a fact that Nishimura was the senior officer in question. In face of the evidence, it is likely that he will admit guilt by offering the defence of a 'mercy-killing'. Failing this, he will be in such a position that he must disclose the names of subordinate formations and commanders, from whom the necessary evidence should be obtainable.

2. Lieutenant-General Renya Mutaguchi, GOC 18th Division.

That the Japanese were officially aware of the Alexandra Hospital massacre is proved by the visit of a senior officer on 16 February 1942 to apologise (ref. the Red Cross Senior Representative's statement). It was after I had mentioned this to General Yamashita that he gave me Mutaguchi's name, agreeing that this officer was probably a member of Mutaguchi's staff.

3. Lieutenant-General Fukuye, GOC Allied prisoners-of-war Malaya, August to December 1942.

101

The case against Fukuye is that he was responsible for the shooting at Changi on 2 September 1942 of Cpl Breavington and three others. This was done as an attempt to terrorise all prisoners into signing the illegal 'non-escape form', or 'parole' as the Japs chose to call it. Breavington and one other were brought from the prison hospital in their pyjamas. It is believed that none of these men had been tried by a military court. Under interrogation the interpreter, Koroyasu, who witnessed the execution, recently stated that Fukuye ordered it. Capt. Rana, INA, who commanded the firing-squad of Indians with obvious relish and himself fired, was recently arrested at Delhi. Capt. Okasaki, who superintended, is still at large.

4. Major-General Arimura, GOC Allied prisoners-of-war Malaya December 1942 to January 1944.

Arimura was largely responsible for the death of 4,000 British and Australian troops in Thailand during May to December 1943, as F and H Forces, to which they belonged, remained under his administration during this period in Thailand. Some points for interrogation are:

(i) Why was F Force ordered to make up its numbers to 7,000 by including 2,000 unfit men?

(ii) Why did his staff state that F Force would not be used for labour but was destined for 'health-camps' where the food would be much better? (Any man who could stand was made to work and all were on starvation rations.)

(iii) Why were we told that there would be no marching, and that any sick man should be included in F Force who could stand four days in a train and a short journey by lorry? (All men were compelled to march 200 miles at night in 2½ weeks along jungle-tracks during the monsoon-rains.)

(iv) Why were the huts not roofed in any of the labour-camps until after the troops of F Force had arrived?

(v) Lack of drugs and dressings: gross ill-treatment of the men at work.

(vi) Forced labour of several hundred officers of H Force in railway-construction gangs.

(vii) Forced labour of Medical Officers and Orderlies of K and L Forces, which were medical parties sent to Thailand by Arimura to look after the conscripted native labourers.

Orders and promises contained in (i), (ii), and (iii) above were given to me personally, as Colonel Holmes's representative, by Arimura's staff at Changi before I left for Thailand with F Force in April 1943.

signed: C.H.D. Wild, Major for O C 'E' GROUP (SOUTH)
SINGAPORE 9 November 1945

Lieutenant-General Tomoyuki Yamashita was sentenced to death by the American War Crimes Tribunal in Manila on 7 December 1945, his crime principally 'command responsibility' for the crimes of subordinates. He was hanged on 23 February 1946.

NOTES

[1] Allied Land Forces South-East Asia

[2] See page 104

[3] Major-General Kojima was GOC *Kempeitai* in Singapore, Malaya, S. Siam and S. Burma.

[4] Private Colin F. Brien was captured on 26 February 1942. On 1 March, his hands bound, he was taken into a jungle clearing where a platoon of soldiers, 12 officers and a freshly dug shallow grave awaited him. Brien later testified at the IMTFE (International Military Tribunal for the Fast-East), Tokyo:

'I was told to sit down with my knees, legs and feet projecting into the grave. My hands were tied behind my back. A small towel was tied over my eyes, and then my shirt was unbuttoned and pulled back over my back, exposing the lower part of my neck. My head was bent forward, and after a few seconds I felt a heavy, dull blow sensation on the back of my neck. I realised I was still alive, but pretended to be dead and fell over on my right side: after that I lost consciousness.'

When he awoke Brien found he was at the bottom of the grave, with wooden pilings and clods of earth on top of him. His hands were still tied behind his back and he was drenched in blood. He lay there for about an hour before managing to dislodge the debris with his feet. He crawled out and hid in a nearby patch of *lalang* grass but was, inevitably, recaptured. The amazed Japanese put him in a hospital and he survived the war in a POW camp.

[5] SSVF – Straits Settlement Volunteer Force

[6] FMSVF – Federated Malay States Volunteer Force

[7] See page 100

Ref.	Date	Area	Outline of Charge
2	22.1.42	Yong Peng, Johore.	Presumed shooting of L/Sgt Keiller, AIF, while sick and a prisoner.
1	22.1.42	Parit Sulong Village, Muar, Johore.	Torture, machine-gunning and burning alive with petrol of 110 Australians and 35/40 Indians, being wounded POWs. (Statement of sole survivor, Lt Hackney, 2/29 Bn, confirmed by discovery of victims' remains.)
1	20.1.42	Muar-Parit Sulong Rd., Muar.	Beheading of 200 Australian and Indian POWs. (Statement by 2 Indian OR survivors, confirmed by discovery of victims' remains.)
3	14/15.2.42	Alexandra Hospital, Singapore.	(a) Murder of MOs, orderlies and wounded inside hospital on occupation by the Jap forces. (b) Murder of large number of MOs, orderlies and wounded taken from hospital as prisoners. (Total approx. 20 MOs, 60 orderlies and 200 wounded.)
	15.2.42	Singapore	Shooting of 8 Australian *ex* St Patrick's Hospital, 3 SS Volunteers and a number of European and Indian civilians, all being prisoners (statement by sole survivor, Cpl Croft, 2/30 Bn).
4	19.2.42	Bukit Timah, Singapore.	Shooting of 14 Australian prisoners off Reformatory Road, Bukit Timah, after they had been held as POWs at Jap HQ Pasir Panjang, since 16 Feb. (Statement by Pte Alf McCann, the sole survivor.)
	1.3.42	Singapore	Attempted execution by beheading and partial burial of Pte Brien, 2/19 Bn, AIF, after he had been held by the enemy as a wounded POW since 26 Feb. (Statement by Pte Brien, supported by medical evidence.)
5	24.2(?).42	Changi, Singapore.	Mass execution of 140 Chinese by machine-gun fire on Changi beach, many of them being members of SSVF.[5] (Statement by survivor and by POW burial party and others.)
5	16 – 20.2(?).42	Off Blakang Mati Island, Singapore.	Mass execution of large numbers of Chinese on several successive days, taken out to sea in launches and machine-gunned in the water. (Statement by Major Smith, FMSVF,[6] a witness.)

Chapter 8
WAR CRIMES – I

Cyril finally reached home in December 1945, and what a time of year to arrive in England after five and a half years in the tropical sun! However, I feel sure that the English wintry weather was the last thing on his mind. He was at last reunited with Celia and his family, the war having treated them all in diverse ways. Apart from the occasional leave from Japan, he had lived away from home for fourteen years.

Celia and Cyril spent much of the next two months with Dr and Mrs Waterhouse at Boar's Hill, Oxford, apart from a few days with David and Mary at Eton, and two rather unsuccessful weeks in London, just before returning to Singapore, when they were both laid up with 'flu.

Cyril had been summoned to the War Crimes Headquarters in London soon after his return home, as the authorities there wanted him to carry on with his work in Malaya. He really was the only man for the job. Obviously the War Office had access to first class interpreters, but none had the advantage of knowing and being able to identify so many of the Japanese suspects, or indeed of having suffered personally at their hands. He therefore felt it his duty to remain in the Army and return to Singapore, but made two conditions. The first was that, after five years' separation he should be allowed to take Celia with him, and the second that he should be made up to a rank from which he could speak to his American counterparts on equal terms, as they were mostly more senior to his rank of major.

Both these stipulations were met and, after a short leave, he returned on 16 February 1946 with Celia, and with the rank of full Colonel, to take up the appointment of War Crimes Liaison Officer, Malaya and Singapore. In this post he controlled the work of the three War Crimes Investigation Teams then operating in that area and, in addition, did valuable work on his own account to produce evidence against Japanese responsible for the deaths of over 3,000 Allied prisoners-of-war of F Force on the Burma-Siam railway. Major interrogations were carried out by him all over the country, as a result of which the War Crimes organisation was able to substantiate numerous charges against

Japanese war criminals and also obtain information of great historical and intelligence value.

Cyril's first letter to David after his return to Singapore described their enjoyable and relaxed six-day journey by Sunderland flying-boat. They spent their first night in a 'pleasant little French country-inn among the pinewoods' near Bordeaux and their second in a house-boat on the Nile. The third night they slept comfortably in the flying-boat, after brief refuelling stops at Habbaniyah and Bahrein, followed by breakfast and shopping in Karachi. After a second night in the air they landed on the Hooghly River at Calcutta and lunched on another house-boat. The fifth night was spent in Rangoon, before the final leg to Singapore and Raffles Hotel, where they made their home for the duration of Cyril's tour of duty with War Crimes.

It was a peaceful way to travel, with no hassle in crowded airports, and certainly a contrast for Cyril to be at Raffles Hotel, so near to River Valley, Havelock Road and even Changi! They were both to be very happy in Singapore and enjoy living there.

> The work is great fun, and just what I wanted. I am officially War Crimes Liaison Officer to *both* Malaya Command (Kuala Lumpur) – Lt-Gen. Sir Frank Masservy – and Singapore District – Major-General Cox. But in addition I liaise with ALFSEA (Massey) and SACSEA (Supremo). Also, I am in charge of *all* War Crimes Investigations in Malaya and Singapore, and have under my command three investigation teams, each under a Lt-Col, situated at Singapore, Kuala Lumpur and Penang. The OC of my Singapore team, incidentally, is James Kilburn of the 52nd. In addition, I frequently have to give evidence at trials in Singapore!

The first trial in which Cyril gave evidence after his appointment as War Crimes Liaison Officer was that of Lt-Gen. Shimpei Fukuye, the Japanese officer in charge of prisoners-of-war in Malaya and Sumatra at the time of the Selerang Incident, an account of which has been given in Chapter 4. The trial took place from 22 to 28 February. The President was Lt-Col S.C. Silkin, RA, of the Middle Temple, and the Prosecutor was Col J. Davies, Dept of Judge Advocate General in India. There were two charges:

1st Charge: Committing a war crime in that he at Changi between 29 August 1942 and 6 September 1942, in violation of the laws and usages of war, was concerned in an attempt to compel POWs in his custody and under his command to sign documents which bound them under oath to refrain from attempts to escape and, in order to enforce such compulsion, was concerned in the ill-treatment of the said POWs and in the removal of more than 15,000 of them to Selerang Barracks where no provision was made for their maintenance and comfort.

2nd Charge: Committing a war crime in that he at Changi on or about 2 September 1942, in violation of the laws and usages of war, was concerned in the killing of Cpl Breavington, Private Gale, Private Walters and Private Fletcher, at that time prisoners-of-war in his custody and under his command.

Fukuye was found guilty and on 28 February 1946 was sentenced to death by shooting. On 12 March he made a 'humble petition', an extract of which reads:

> The defence of the petitioner to the first charge was that the attempt to compel the prisoners-of-war to sign the documents which bound them under oath not to attempt to escape was in accordance with orders from the Minister of War in Tokyo. He alleged further that the concentration of the POWs was the suggestion of Col Holmes, the POW Commander, and that the prisoners were returned to their former quarters after four days.
>
> His defence to the second charge was a complete denial of knowledge or of responsibility for the execution. He stated that it was organised and carried out by his subordinates without his authority.

There was no direct evidence, in fact, that Fukuye had ordered the shooting. However, it is hard to believe that he knew nothing of it since Lt Akira Okasaki, who directed the execution, was his adjutant at that time, acting under his orders, and was in daily contact with him. The venue of the execution was only half a mile from his HQ and was attended by 25 to 30 Japanese officers, including a senior officer of the 25th Army, so his plea of ignorance was clearly preposterous.

Also in his petition Fukuye claimed he received four letters of thanks from Lady Heath, Colonel Holmes and Colonel Craven within 3 1/2 months while he was commander of POWs. 'May your Petitioner humbly point out that these letters would indicate the passion for righteousness, the esteem for humanity and the gentlemanship for which your Petitioner has always tried to stand.' The reference to Lady Heath was intended to try and absolve himself from blame for the fact that Lady Heath had given birth to a stillborn son in Changi Gaol, having had totally inadequate nourishment and attention.

Major-General L.H. Cox, GOC Singapore District, asked Cyril for a confidential report on the condemned prisoner, and Cyril wrote as follows:

CONFIDENTIAL
HQ Allied Land Forces, South-East Asia
5 April 1946

To: General Officer Commanding Singapore District

Lt-Gen. Shimpei Fukuye

1. I have given careful thought to the question of what can be said in favour of Lt-Gen. Shimpei Fukuye; the answer is practically nothing.

2. The measures which he introduced on becoming GOC Prisoners-of-War Malaya in August 1942 were, *at the best*, such as any officer in charge of POWs would have been expected to take, e.g. the compilation of nominal rolls and a card-index; and even this work was bungled.

3. Some of his measures increased the hardship and discomfort of the POWs, e.g. the reduction of accommodation at Changi, causing serious overcrowding, and the added severity of the guards.

4. It was mentioned in his favour in court that he had supplied drugs and medical stores to Changi camp and that he had received a letter of thanks from the British SMO. The answer is: (a) it was his duty to supply medical stores; (b) the amounts received were wholly inadequate at a time when Singapore still contained very large stocks of British medical supplies; (c) when British officers did not write letters of thanks they used to be ordered to do so by the Japanese.

5. The consensus of opinion among all ranks was undoubtedly that Fukuye did even less to ameliorate the condition of POWs than either of his two successors.

signed: C.H.D. Wild
Colonel, War Crimes Liaison Officer

The following day Major-General Cox dismissed the petition and confirmed the sentence:

CONFIDENTIAL
HQ Singapore District, SEAC
6 April 1946

Lt-Gen. Shimpei Fukuye

On the recommendation of the President of the Court, by whom this Japanese War Criminal was tried, I made comprehensive investigations into the man's character and record of service. The attached letter from Col C.H.D. Wild, War Crimes Liaison Officer to Malaya Command and Singapore District, shows that there are no apparent reasons why the sentence of death by shooting should be commuted.

Consequently, I have confirmed the sentence and dismissed his petition.

signed: L.H. Cox
Major-General
Commanding, Singapore District

The shooting imposed on Fukuye, who was 57 at the time, was put into execution at Changi on 27 April 1946, on exactly the same spot where the four prisoners were shot, but in a humane way.

On 15 May Cyril wrote again to David from War Crimes HQ, ALFSEA, Singapore:

> War Crimes are going quite well, the main trouble at the moment being that we cannot get the accommodation to try the little brutes in. We have, however, tried about 170 of them so far, of whom about 70 have been sentenced to death, which is not a bad start.
>
> ... I have my main office in Fort Canning, the HQ Singapore District, but I spend a good deal of my time touring up-country, staying generally with my teams at Kuala Lumpur and Penang, and travelling either by car or air. Also I have made one trip to Bangkok and enjoyed seeing Siam more comfortably than on my last visit. Celia has been a great success in her job, as a Staff Captain in the Legal Dept, which she performs at the main War Crimes camp of ALFSEA at Goodwood Park Hotel. We shall meet in Court shortly – she as assistant to her boss, Lt-Col Couch, and I as a witness in a Burma-Siam railway case. I frequently have to appear as a witness and generally enjoy it, especially when the Jap defence counsel get up to cross-examine.
>
> In the famous Double Tenth case I gave evidence regarding some very damaging admissions made to me by a Jap *kempei* last October. Having a bad foot I had hobbled into Court on a stick and been given a seat in front of the witness-box. A nasty little Jap lawyer, with his spectacles tied together behind his head with a bootlace, got up to cross-examine.
>
> *Jap*: "And when you questioned Makizono in prison, Colonel Wild, had you got that stick with you?"
>
> *Self*: "No".
>
> *Jap*: "Had you any other stick with you?"
>
> *Self*: "No."
>
> *Jap*: (triumphantly) "And how long have you had that stick?"
>
> *Self*: "My wife bought it for me at lunch-time."
>
> (Makizono was sentenced to be hanged for torture and murder.)

Cyril investigated the Double Tenth case in great detail and, as well as giving evidence at the trials in Singapore, he also gave evidence for the prosecution when this case was cited in the Major War Crimes Tribunal in Tokyo in September. In September 1943 the Japanese had become hypersensitive and imagined that there was an active spy ring operating throughout prisoner-of-war and civilian internee camps. They carried out intensive searches, particularly among the civilian men interned in Changi Gaol, although three of the women there were also 'suspect'.

Without doubt the main reason for this uneasiness amongst the Japanese was Colonel Ivan Lyon's successful (and as far as the Japanese were concerned, unresolved) sea operation, 'Jaywick', when 40,000 tons of enemy shipping, including a tanker, were sunk in Keppel Harbour. The Japanese authorities believed an unfounded report that this attack had been mounted by British servicemen still at large in Johore, and that they were being fed information through short-wave radio transmitters in Changi Gaol. Other factors contributing to this Japanese alert may have been the discovery of the radio at Kanchanaburi at approximately the same time, and perhaps also the recapture of the survivors of my own escape party from the railway. They could not believe that we had crossed the mountainous jungle country between the Three Pagodas Pass and the coast of Tavoy and, at first, thought we must have been parachuted in to the Burma coast. The day fixed for our proposed execution was 9 October 1943.

Whatever the reasons, on 10 October 1943 (the tenth day of the tenth month) Japanese *Kempeitai* arrested for questioning people whom they thought might be implicated in this imaginary spy-ring. Included amongst them were The Right Reverend Leonard Wilson, Bishop of Singapore, and Hugh Fraser, former Colonial Secretary who, with Cyril, had made the first contact with the enemy before the surrender negotiations on 15 February 1942. Amongst the 45 civilians arrested were Freddy Bloom, married for just nine days before capitulation to Philip Bloom, a doctor in the British Army, Dr Cicely Williams and a young Chinese woman, Elizabeth Choy. Elizabeth Choy's husband, who had a shop in the Tan Tock Seng Hospital, was also arrested, accused of sending wireless parts and money for internees into Changi Gaol.

The whole party was taken to the YMCA building and another two-storeyed building in Smith Street where they were crowded into bamboo cage cells, between 15 and 20 to a 'cage'. Each cell was completely bare except for one asiatic squatter latrine, the only source of water for drinking and washing. There was no privacy whatsoever, even for the three women, and they were under the constant watch of guards who walked up and down in the corridor outside the cells. Throughout most of the days and nights individuals were taken out for interrogation and torture, which included the electric and water treatments, stomach stamping, and burning. The sounds of the beatings and the shrieks of those being tortured only subsided when the unconscious and mutilated bodies were dragged back to the cells, after several hours. This horrendous existence dragged on for between five and eight months. Fifteen died as a result of this treatment by the *Kempeitai*, including Hugh Fraser and Adrian Clark, Chief Legal Adviser to the Government. The Bishop, though cruelly beaten and tortured, survived, as did Freddy Bloom, Dr Cicely Williams and Elizabeth Choy who, with her husband, was threatened with immediate execution if she didn't 'confess'. She remains terrified of electricity to this day. Surely there can be no braver people than the survivors of the Double Tenth.

The following extract is taken from a letter written on 21 September 1945 by an Assistant Chief of Staff at the HQ of the Supreme Allied Commander South-East Asia, now in the possession of the Imperial War Museum and the Wild family:

... I met the Bishop of Singapore, a man who looks sixty and whose age is, in fact, 46. I feel it is my duty to tell you a little of this wonderful man, whom I look upon as a modern saint.

During the occupation he was initially allowed his freedom, and he did much to help the Chinese population and, when allowed, the British internees as well. He kept the cathedral open and never a day passed without a service being held.

... The Japanese looked round for a scapegoat, and because the Bishop was a more or less free man and had ample opportunity for being involved in subversive activities, the *Kempeitai* arrested him and took him to their HQ. He remained there for nearly a year, locked in a small cell some six feet by four. He was deprived of his clothes, except for a pair of shorts, and he had no toothbrush, soap, shaving material, etc. during the whole of his time there. I do not want to go into too much detail over the tortures which that man suffered during the time, but I would like just to tell you what he said about the first four days.

On the first day they took him out, tied his hands behind his back, made him kneel on the floor and then beat him with rope ends across his back for eight hours, the beaters working in shifts. He was then thrown back into the cell and left till the following day.

The next day he was removed and again his hands were tied behind him. Three steel bars (not rounded) were placed behind his knees and he was then made to sit on his heels for six hours. Heavy weights were dropped on to his thighs and Japanese soldiers jumped on him. You can appreciate the agony of this torture when you think of steel bars being forced into the back of your legs by pressure being placed on your thighs. The Bishop said he could not walk afterwards, but was made to drag himself along to his cell.

On the third day they took him out, tied him to a table with his head hanging over the end without any support. He was then beaten for six hours from the stomach downwards with bamboo rods. You will see the brutality of this torture, with his head pumping away madly, and the blood being slowly drained out of the lower limbs. The object of these barbaric acts was to make him confess that he was the head of the spy organisation.

Perhaps the worst torture that he suffered was on the fourth day, for they placed him on a table, again bound in a similar manner, and put a wet rag across his face and into his mouth. The Chief of Police then interrogated him; if he refused to answer he was beaten with rods. Every time he opened his mouth to speak water was poured on to the rags and into his mouth, and of course he was forced to swallow it. By this means they filled him up until his belly became distended and water poured out of his body from every point possible. Then they beat his distended belly with bamboo rods for six hours and finally threw him back into his cell.

I have since seen an officer of one of HM ships who saw his body naked when he was brought on board to be given a bath; you would not believe a man with such horrible sores, such deep scars, and such rents in his flesh, could ever live.

During those months he was held by the *Kempeitai* he was frequently beaten, and he said that God mercifully granted him oblivion after he had counted up to 200 strokes at any one time. General Kimmins asked him whether he cursed the Japanese during his sufferings, and whether he had hatred in his soul as a result of all he had endured. He replied, "Oh no, I never cursed the Japanese. I screamed out several times because, if you forgive my saying so, the pain was too much to endure without screaming. But I prayed to God continuously and God made me realise that the Japanese were his children in spite of all their brutality. They were possibly God's misguided children. I bear them no malice. I am grateful and better for the experience."

That is the story of the Bishop, the most wonderful man I have ever met. His courage and sincerity no-one could doubt. His name is lauded throughout Singapore, and his example is the admiration of the world.

Cyril made the arrests of those *Kempeitai* suspected of being implicated in the Double Tenth massacre, for that was what it amounted to, and collated the evidence against them.

I had the pleasure of parading the catch in front of Bishop Wilson, whom we took to the Central Police Station to identify them. He is a very fine man and shows no sign of his appalling 8-months ordeal. I found that he is an old friend of John's and looks forward to seeing him soon. The contrast between his dignified bearded figure and the sub-human troglodytes who had nearly tortured him to death was very striking. He was much too gentle with them, but some had the grace to look ashamed of themselves.

Twenty-six defendants were tried by the War Crimes Court held in the Supreme Court Building, Singapore, from 18 March to 15 April 1946. The President of the Court was Lt-Col S.C. Silkin, RA. Six of the defendants were acquitted on the grounds of mistaken identity or insufficient evidence. Two were sentenced to eight years' imprisonment, one to fifteen years and three to life imprisonment. The remaining fourteen, including Sgt-Major Makizono (mentioned earlier in connection with the walking-stick episode) were sentenced to die by hanging.

Cyril concluded his letter of 15 May to David:

> I am very glad to hear that Mary is doing so well. Please give her my love. It was fun having those few days with you at Eton before we started back, and something to which I had been looking forward for so long.
>
> We have quite comfortable quarters here in the Raffles Hotel, which I always thought a greatly overrated place and which was not improved by 3¹/₂ years of Japanese neglect. However, it suits us very well, and it would certainly not have been worthwhile hunting for a house and then for furniture and servants, all at fantastic prices. Also Celia has a full day without the added bother of housekeeping.
>
> I have no idea how long this job will take. After three months I feel that my own show is running itself, and a steady stream of completed cases will continue to pour in to the Legal Dept for as long as they are prepared to go on trying them. So I see no need to linger on till the bitter end, unless they want to send me on some worthwhile mission elsewhere. If not, I hope that two months or so will see me through.
>
> ... I have just finished a 4-days interrogation of a Jap senior officer connected with the Railway. I staggered him halfway by reminding him that I had met him at Sonkurai camp in October 1943! I did the whole thing myself in Japanese for a mixed team of Australians, Americans and Dutch...
>
> Celia sends her love to you both. So do I.

Your affectionate brother,

Cyril

In June 1946 Cyril wrote to Celia's mother, telling her of his visit to his investigating team based in Penang. His descriptions not only portray the beauty of the island but also give an interesting insight into the situation pertaining in Penang at that time.

> ... They inhabit one of the loveliest houses in Penang, with a very large garden full of trees and flowers and well-stocked with Straits robins, bulbuls and a kingfisher. Behind is the beautiful slope of Penang Peak, jungle-covered and over 2,000 feet high. This is my fourth visit. It is always a joy to come here after the noise and heat of Singapore.

... Meantime, I had been asked to tea with the Governor-General[1]...
Henry Haynes (a Lt-Col commanding the Penang team) and I had the
great man entirely to ourselves for an hour and a half. He *is* a great man,
as one would expect of someone with his record at 44, delightfully informal
and with a very good sense of humour. Much of my work lately has had
a strong political bearing and it was a very great help to be able to talk
things over with HE himself... Also, Henry and I are both in love with
this country and its people, especially in view of the astonishing loyalty
and courage of so many humble folk of all races which our investigations
have brought to light. It is distressing that so many others who collaborated
wholeheartedly with the Japanese have been confirmed in the positions to
which they attained under them. We talked of all this, and found our own
words quoted in Malcolm Macdonald's *Message to Malaya*, which he wrote
later that evening. Best of all, he said, ''Do you think it would be a good
idea if I gave a special party here for these people?'' Of course we were
delighted, the plans were made then and there, and Henry is to provide the
names of all of them, about 400. Henry said, ''Of course many of them will
be the very simplest people, from jungle-villages and grass huts.'' ''Those
are just the people that I want'', he said. There is no doubt that this will
have a wonderful effect throughout the whole country. I have met Malcolm
Macdonald twice since then. I am convinced that he is going to be a glorious
success and that no better man could possibly have been sent here.

Saturday was Victory Day. There was a parade and march-past of a
thousand troops, half British and half Indian. But the highlight of this
parade was the presentation of certificates signed by the Supremo to 40
people who had helped our troops during the Japanese occupation. All
these people had been found and their cases investigated by officers of
this Team. On this Island alone (Penang) there were nearly 20 British
soldiers of the Leicesters and E. Surreys hiding in the hills after being
cut off during our retreat in 1941. They were fed and taken care of by
all sorts of humble folk, mainly Chinese but some Malays and one or two
Indians, at terrible risk to themselves and their families. The astonishing
thing was that when a Chinese was caught by the Japanese and taken off
to be tortured and executed, his next-of-kin used to continue the work of
mercy. The last of these British soldiers was caught by the Japanese a few
weeks before the end of war. He was first tortured and then murdered *after*
the war ended. I have got the Japs who did it. We had been enabled to give
rewards ranging from $500 to $9,000 to these 40 people, but they were
even more pleased with the certificates which the Governor-General gave
them at this parade. Haynes made an excellent speech and then handed the
certificates to the Governor-General, with a word in his ear about the work
of each of them as they came up for the presentation. The first recipients
were five Chinese widows, all of whom had lost their husbands and three
of whom had been themselves tortured for helping our men. This I regard
as the pleasantest side of War Crimes work.

In the afternoon there was a Garden Party at the Residency, where
Malcolm Macdonald is living for the time being. The main feature of
this was a *Chingay*, a festival-procession which streamed up the drive

the Residency for two hours. It was headed by all the school children of Penang, followed by a wonderful assortment of decorated lorries, bullock-carts and even bicycles, lion-dancers, sword-fighters, bands, tumblers, and thousands of Chinese, Malays and Indians walking by villages, communities and streets, each under their own banners and all expressing loyalty to the King and pride in the victory. It was a really wonderful demonstration both of patriotism and of the regained harmony between the different races of Malaya, which the Japs had done their utmost to destroy.

It was a great pity that Celia could not come up with me this time. But I hope to come back with her on a week's leave very soon. She has been a great success in her job and is, in fact, performing the duties of *two* staff-captains! She enjoys the work and I have never seen her in better health and spirits.

In August 1946 Cyril wrote, what appears to be, his last letter to David. In it he said:

I have extracted Celia from her rather circumscribed billet in the Legal Department and made her my new PA. So she now works under my eye in the same room with me in Fort Canning. It is an excellent thing to have her under strict military discipline during working hours, though I have not yet got her to call me ''Sir''!

How is the weight going in austerity-ridden England? The food here is good, except for a great shortage of fresh vegetables, and I am back to within half a stone of normal.

Cyril sought out and apprehended over 170 suspected war criminals, all of whom were brought to trial in Singapore. He gave evidence himself in five of the trials, but his main evidence was used in the Major War Crimes Trials held by the International Military Tribunal for the Far-East (IMTFE) in the War Ministry Building at Ichigaya, Tokyo.

General Douglas MacArthur had promulgated the Charter of the Tribunal on 19 January 1946, and it was convened on 29 April of that year under the presidency of an Australian judge, Sir William Webb, who said at the time, 'There has been no more important criminal trial in all history.' In fact, the Tokyo Trial developed into an enormous affair, completely dwarfing the activities of the more famous Nuremberg Trial. The recorded transcript amounted to 50,000 pages of ten million words, but it has to be said that language difficulties created many lengthy arguments and misunderstandings.

Ichigaya had been the hilltop headquarters for the Japanese military during the war. The spacious auditorium, approximately 100 feet in length, was transformed by the occupation authorities into a courtroom, complete with wood panelling, incandescent floodlights and a glass-enclosed booth for the translators. There were separate sections for the defendants, their lawyers[2], the prosecutors, press, and of course the judges who sat on a raised platform. There was a large balcony at one end for spectators; 200,000 attended the trial, 150,000 of them Japanese. 419 witnesses, including Pu Yi the last Emperor of China, gave evidence and, in addition, 779 affidavits and depositions were introduced. On any given day there were about 1,000 people in court, and seven news agencies had regular correspondents at the trial.

The Japanese public understood that the primary object of the trial was the identification and punishment of the so-called Major War Criminals, but there was a secondary object which was the moral reconstruction of the world in general and of the Japanese nation in particular. It was also recognised that the 28 defendants were representative of those who had taken Japan into war, and that they were certainly not the only alleged war criminals.[3]

It was truly an international tribunal with no less than eleven member countries. India and the Philippines were added to the original nine, which were: Australia, Canada, China, France, the Netherlands, New Zealand, Russia, the United Kingdom, and the United States. These member countries nominated the eleven Judges for the Tribunal.

Earphones were provided for almost everyone in the courtroom as the proceedings took place in both English and Japanese simultaneously and, as the occasion arose, in Chinese, Russian, French and Dutch. Often, when barbaric acts were described by witnesses some of those in the dock removed their headphones. With heads bowed or eyes closed they were unwilling or unable to listen to the evidence.

A film of the trial shows Sir William Webb as softly spoken, yet he intimidated witnesses and especially counsel for the defence, and even his colleagues on the bench, but he felt strongly that no capital sentences should be imposed on any of the defendants.

Those on trial were a reasonable cross-section of the leaders whom the Allied Powers as a whole regarded as responsible for Japanese policy from 1931 until the end of the Pacific War in 1945. No fewer than four of them were *ex*-prime ministers. There was some argument as to whether Emperor Hirohito himself should be arraigned in the dock, but the United States was adamantly against it. Hirohito did, in fact, offer himself for trial 'as the one to bear the sole responsibility for every political and military decision made and action taken by my people in the conduct of the war'. Had his offer been accepted by MacArthur, and Hirohito had shouldered responsibility for the war, then all the other defendants would necessarily have been acquitted.

Prince Fumimaro Konoye, General Shigeru Honjo, General Korechika Anami, Field-Marshal Hajime Sugiyama – and many others – committed suicide before they could be brought to trial. The following 28 defendants were those who, in the end, stood in the dock as Class A war criminals, indicted on 55 counts of crimes against peace, outright murder, and other war crimes:

General Sadaō Araki	Marquis Koichi Kidō
Shumei Okawa	General Kenji Doihara
General Heitarō Kimura	General Hiroshi Ōshima
Colonel Kingorō Hashimoto	General Kuniaki Koisō
General Kenryō Satō	Field-Marshal Shunroku Hata
General Iwane Matsui	Mamuru Shigemitsu
Baron Kiichirō Hiranuma	Yosuke Matsuoka
Admiral Shigetarō Shimada	Baron Kōki Hirota
General Jirō Minami	Toshiō Shiratori
Naoki Hoshinō	General Akira Mutō
Shigenori Tōgō	Okinori Kaya
General Teiichi Suzuki	General Seishirō Itagaki
Admiral Osami Naganō	General Hideki Tōjō
General Yoshijirō Umezu	Admiral Takasumi Ōka

By the time Cyril arrived in Tokyo the Tribunal had been in session for over four months. Cyril's testimony was given out of turn, from 11 to 19 September, his time in Tokyo being limited as he was urgently required for other trials in his home base of Singapore. Sir Arthur Comyns Carr was the British Associate Prosecutor and Mr Joseph B. Keenan, an American, was Chief Prosecutor. The prosecution had the benefit of 84 lawyers, whereas the defence relied on 150 lawyers.

Cyril took the witness stand on *11 September 1946*. Mr Keenan's request to present the witness out of order was granted, Sir Arthur Comyns Carr established Cyril's credentials and then proceeded with his direct examination.

MR COMYNS CARR:

Q   'Now, since your captivity came to an end and the Japanese surrendered, has it been part of your duty as a war crimes investigation officer to investigate these matters from that end?'

A   'Yes, it has been since the first of September 1945.'

Q 'Now, since the surrender, have you and your colleagues made an investigation of this matter of the slaughter of Chinese in Singapore, about which you have told us one part already – one part about which you were present at the complaint?'

A 'It is a case which I, or officers under my command, have been investigating the last year.'

Q 'Can you say how many Chinese were slaughtered by the Japanese immediately after the surrender?'

A 'Yes. I can. The number was definitely considerably in excess of 5,000 men.'

Cyril went on to confirm that there was no fighting in the streets of Singapore city and, at the time the surrender was signed, three Japanese divisions were on the outskirts of the city waiting to assault it. None of these divisions ever entered the city, on General Yamashita's orders. The only troops to be allowed in were the *Kempeitai*[4] (Military Police) and the *Keibaitai* (Garrison Troops). Order was maintained under the terms of the surrender by 500 armed British troops until the Japanese took over the city in the early morning of 16 February.

Afternoon Session of 11 September

MR COMYNS CARR:

Q 'Colonel Wild, when the Tribunal adjourned you were just beginning to tell us about a report made out by Major Bull. What was that about?'

A 'It was about a massacre at the Alexandra Hospital on Singapore Island on 14 and 15 February 1942.'

Q 'Tell us what he said.'

Cyril then gave a report on that frightful massacre and, in answer to questions from Sir Arthur Comyns Carr, he told of a further massacre in January 1942 of 110 Australians and 35 to 40 Indians at Parit Sulong. Both of these have already been described in the previous chapter, but the questioning on the Parit Sulong massacre concluded:

Q 'Since the Japanese surrender have the remains of these unfortunate men been found in the place described by Lieutenant Hackney?'

A 'On the strength of what Lieutenant Hackney told me, I arranged for a search party to go out to the place which he had indicated. They found the remains of these men there. They had not been buried.'

There appears to be no chronological or obvious reason for the order in which Sir Arthur Comyns Carr questioned Cyril in his direct examination. This could have been due partly to the fact that Cyril's time in Tokyo was limited owing to his commitments to the Singapore trials, in which he was often the key witness for the prosecution. However, Arnold C. Brackman, an American, who was a press reporter present at the Tribunal, writes in his book *The Other Nuremberg*:

... Too often, the evidence bogged down in such arcane matters as interpretations of the Japanese Constitution. The drama inherent in the situation was often dissipated in a blur of legalistic manoeuvres.

In the end, it seems to me virtually impossible to write a chronological history of the trial without having witnessed it. To observe the trial was as necessary as studying the picture on the box of a jigsaw puzzle before starting to put it together. For there were indeed many and varied pieces. Both the prosecution and defence, sometimes for reasons beyond their control, called witnesses out of turn, introduced evidence out of sequence, and went off on tangents unrelated to the testimony at hand...

The defence, which included both Japanese and American lawyers, was often deliberately obstructive... Thus, much of the court's time – perhaps more than a third – was taken up by motions, briefs, and interminable arguments over what seemed to most of us rather fine points of law.

MR COMYNS CARR:

Q 'Now another subject: In May 1942 did Colonel Heath, whom you have mentioned before, arrive at River Valley Camp from Changi?'

A 'Yes, he did.'

Q 'Did he inform you of the matter concerning three gunners of his regiment?'

A 'Yes, he did.'

Q 'Will you tell us about that?'

A 'Lieutenant-Colonel Heath told me that in March 1942 he had been ordered by the Japanese to attend the execution of three men of his own regiment.'

119

Q   'What did the Japanese say they were going to be executed for?'

A   'The Japanese said that they had captured these three men in Johore while attempting to escape and had brought them back to Singapore. Lieutenant-Colonel Heath told me that Lieutenant-General Percival made a very strong protest to the Japanese, telling them that this proposed execution was illegal.'

Q   'What had happened in the end?'

A   'Colonel Heath, with some other British officers, was taken to the beach outside Changi camp. He was allowed to speak to these three gunners of his for a moment or two. His three men were then shot in front of Colonel Heath by the Japanese.'

Q   'Did he give you the names of these three men?'

A   'He did. I can remember one at the moment, McCann.'

Cyril then went on to explain, in answer to questions from Sir Arthur Comyns Carr, how at River Valley Road they had been ordered to sign a 'parole' promising not to escape, but had refused as such a document would be illegal. He told of how he and Colonel Heath were allowed to go to Changi to confer with Lt-Col Holmes, and went on to describe the 'Selerang Incident'. He confirmed that he had given evidence at the trial of Lieutenant-General Fukuye some months previously.

Sir Arthur moved on to the 'Double Tenth' episode. At the time it occurred Cyril was on the railway at Sonkurai, but at the end of the war he investigated the case in close detail.[5] By this time the defendants had all been tried in minor war crimes courts in Singapore; nevertheless, Sir Arthur Comyns Carr wanted the whole incident to be recounted at the Tokyo Tribunal, and Cyril complied with this request.

The next subject for attention was the appalling treatment meted out by the *Kempeitai* in Outram Road Gaol which, prior to the war, had been the civilian gaol for Singapore.

MR COMYNS CARR:

Q   'Now will you tell us about Outram Road Gaol in Singapore?'

A   'Outram Road Gaol was the military prison of the Japanese forces in and around Singapore.'

Q   'What were you able to find out as to the conditions in Outram Road Prison?'

A   'The British and Allied prisoners in Outram Road Prison were made to sit at attention in their cells for about fourteen hours a day, and at night they had to lie down under a naked electric bulb.[6] The food which they received was grossly inadequate and far less than that given to the Japanese prisoners. Japanese convicts were employed as warders over the prisoners-of-war. They were frequently beaten up.'

Q   'With regard to medical attention, what happened?'

A   'They got no medical attention whatever unless they were practically in a dying condition.'

Q   'Were any of them ever released owing to sickness?'

A   'When they were desperately ill they were sent out to Changi camp to be put into the prisoner-of-war hospital there. Altogether about a hundred came out during the three and one-half years.'

Q   'Did the Japanese medical officers visit those men while they were there frequently?'

A   'Every two months or so they would be visited in the special ward where they were kept.'

Q   'For what purpose?'

A   'To see if they had recovered sufficiently to go back to Outram Road Gaol.'

Q   'Were there large numbers of deaths in the gaol?'

A   'On the civilian side of the gaol, very many. In the military side: not so many in the gaol, but a number of them died after they came out to Changi.'[7]

Q   'Since the Japanese surrender, have a considerable number of those who were employed in Outram Road Gaol, the Commandant and medical officers and so on, been brought to trial?'

A   'About forty-four of them are now on trial, I understand.'

Q   'Now, did you personally in about June 1944 see some of these men brought to Changi from Outram Road Gaol?'

A 'Yes, I did.'

Q 'Describe it.'

A 'Four men arrived in a bus from Outram Road Gaol under a Japanese escort. I was called by the Japanese to receive them. I lifted all four out of the bus myself.'

Q 'What was their condition?'

A 'They were so thin that it was difficult to believe that they could still be alive. They seemed to weigh only a few stone when I picked them up.'

Q 'Could they speak?'

A 'Only in a feeble whisper.'

Q 'What nationalities were these four men?'

A 'Two were Dutch and two were British.'

Q 'What became of them?'

A 'Two of them died within the next two or three days.'

Q 'Was there a post-mortem report by an Australian medical officer?'

A 'Yes, he showed it to me. He mentioned in it that their bowels were as thin as tissue paper from starvation.'

Q 'When you lifted the four men out of the bus, did you notice anything else there?'

A 'Yes, a rough wooden box.'

Q 'What was in the box?'

A 'I lifted the lid and there was an elderly European, the dead body of an elderly European in it.'

Q 'What did you notice about the condition of that?'

A 'He had a white beard. He was very thin, and his knees were drawn up and his hands were clasped across his stomach.'

Sir Arthur Comyns Carr had no further questions for Cyril on this subject at this juncture, and the court adjourned until the following morning.

NOTES

1 Malcolm Macdonald, son of Ramsay Macdonald

2 This was unlike the Japanese legal system which did not permit defendants to have defence lawyers. (Ref. my own trial, p. 58)

3 It was intended to hold further war crimes trials, and in fact the Allied Powers prosecuted no less than 5,570 minor war criminals. 80% were found guilty and about 1,000 were executed. Many who would have been tried committed suicide after the surrender broadcast.

4 Major General Kojima was GOC *Kempeitai* in Singapore, Malaya, S. Siam and S. Burma – the 'Himmler of Malaya'.

5 See page 109

6 The sole items in these cells were two bare planks to lie on at night, one block of wood (without curved edges) for a pillow, one blanket for use at night, and one latrine bucket. The author was one of the few to be in solitary confinement; most of the others in the military side of the gaol were in pairs. The size of each cell on the military side was 11' 0" x 5' 6" x 11' 3" at the highest point.

7 Actual deaths in the gaol totalled 1,283. Many went mad.

Chapter 9

WAR CRIMES – II

The Tribunal resumed on *Thursday 12 September 1946*, and Sir Arthur Comyns Carr began by asking Cyril to tell the Court about the building of the Burma-Siam Railway and what purpose it served. Having been described in detail in Chapter 4, it would be repetitive to quote Cyril's testimony here, but one additional point of interest came to light. This was the fact that at Sonkurai the Japanese would not accept a death certificate giving dysentery as the cause of death. They insisted on new certificates, giving diarrhoea as the cause of death. When asked the reason for this compulsory alteration, the Japanese interpreter of F Force said that in the Japanese army it was regarded as a disgrace to the administration and to the medical services if men in their charge died of infectious diseases. This is incredible when one reflects on the instances when the Japanese deliberately placed prisoners-of-war next to infectious cases, as at Selerang and on the march up to the railway.[1]

Cyril stressed the fact that 1,600 men had marched in to Sonkurai early in May 1943 of whom 1,200 were dead by November.

Q   'In September of that year, did you receive an order from a Japanese officer about that camp?'

A   'I was told that as we were preventing more than 200 men from going out to work each day, we had to evacuate the whole of a long hut within four days.'

Q   'What was to happen to the sick who were still there?'

A   '700 men were to be put out into the jungle.'

Q   'Did he tell you why?'

A   'Because the hut was to be filled up with Asiatic coolies, because they could do the work.'

Q   'Was that, in fact, done or did you succeed in preventing it?'

A   'The Asiatic coolies did, in fact, arrive at the time stated, but I succeeded in preventing it.'[2]

This order to expel 700 sick prisoners-of-war into the jungle to die had already been endorsed by Colonel Banno's administration. After the Singapore trials in September and October 1946 Banno was sentenced to three years' imprisonment, a somewhat lenient sentence. The fact that he had finally prevented the execution of the four survivors of my escape attempt proved to be a mitigating influence. Cyril had said, 'I personally was always treated by him with civility. I shall say what I can in his favour when he comes up for trial in Singapore very shortly.' When asked whether Banno indicated a desire to cooperate with Cyril in his work, he had replied, 'I can't say that I ever got that impression, but he was not hostile to me in any way and, in some ways, quite friendly.' An ageing, grey-haired man, Banno was just thoroughly ineffective.

The questioning continued:

Q   'What was the work which was supposed to be done at this camp?' (Sonkurai)

A   'It consisted chiefly of building a high level, heavy timber bridge across a river gorge. Also, building the embankments and digging the cuttings and approaches to it. The timber we felled and moved ourselves.'

Q   'How many prisoners-of-war died over that job?'

A   'I should say that that bridge cost a thousand British lives.

Q   'Do you remember an incident about a cook?'

A   'Yes. I was called out of my hut and saw one of our British cooks sitting on the ground with his head laid open. He had been struck on the head with an axe by a Japanese guard.'

Q   'Did you make a complaint about that?'

A   'I went and fetched a Japanese officer and showed him both the wounded man, the axe and the Japanese who had done it.'

Q   'What happened?'

A   'The Japanese officer said very mildly to the Japanese, "That does not do." The guard was not punished.'

125

Q   'Do you remember the circumstances of an escape from Sonkurai camp and what happened about it afterwards?'

A   'Eight British officers escaped from Sonkurai camp in July 1943. They had agreed to risk their lives in order to tell the outside world of the treatment we were getting. They were captured after 52 days in the jungle, during which five of them died. They were brought back to Sonkurai camp and I was told to go to see them shot. I protested about that and they were sent to Singapore, where they were sentenced to 9 and 8 years' penal servitude.'[3]

Q   'Was that after you, yourself, had returned to Singapore?'

A   'Yes, that trial took place after I had returned.'

Q   'At the end of the war were those men released with others from Outram Road Gaol?'

A   'One was released from Outram Gaol. The others had all been brought back to Changi camp as seriously ill.'

Q   'Was there any difference in their treatment in Outram Gaol from what you have described already with regard to other prisoners?'

A   'Their treatment was exactly the same except that one, who had dozens of ulcers on his legs and could only walk with crutches at the time I saw him. He told me that the bandages were removed as soon as he was put in his cell and that he got no medical treatment during his imprisonment.'[4]

When the Tribunal met, pursuant to adjournment, at 9.30 a.m. on *Friday 13 September* Sir Arthur Comyns Carr read from a Japanese document from 'Chief of Prisoner-of-War Camps in Siam' to 'Chief of Prisoner-of-War Information Bureau'. The subject was: Information *re*: British prisoners-of-war in Burma:

> At that time provisions and rations were scarce, quarters and establishments were poor and medical facilities were inadequate. Moreover, for strategic reasons, it was necessary to complete the railway by August 1943 and the work was pushed forward at a terrific pace, with the result that many prisoners-of-war became ill and many died.
>
> Following the opening of the railway to traffic in October 1943 all prisoners-of-war in Burma were concentrated in Kanchanaburi, Nong Pladuk and Thā Makham, except a few who were to assist the Railway Unit. Both the quarter facilities and provisions have been improved at present and both the number of patients and deaths have decreased considerably.

Cyril was questioned about the figures given for the numbers employed on the railway and the numbers of casualties, which he confirmed were broadly accurate.

The prosecution then considered another report *re*: British prisoners-of-war in Burma, but this time from the 'Commander of Southern Army Field Railway Unit'. This unit must surely bear the major responsibility for the maltreatment of prisoners and coolies working on the railway. It was the engineers who constantly drove men far beyond their human capacity.

Since the proposed site of the railway line was a virgin jungle, shelter, food provisions and medical supplies were far from adequate and much different from normal conditions for prisoners-of-war. During the rainy season of 1943 transportation was frequently interrupted and both Japanese soldiers and prisoners-of-war were obliged to put up with much hardship. The Japanese Army Medical Corps tried in vain to stem the violent outbreak of malaria and sickness of digestive organs. However, with the opening of the said railway in October 1943 both the number of patients and deaths diminished with the completion of provisions and facilities.

Q   'Colonel Wild, what do you say about the efforts there alleged of the Japanese Army Medical Corps to stem the violent outbreak of disease?'

A   'I saw no signs of them.'

The Tribunal moved on to the report of the Japanese Government on the Burma-Siam Railway, exhibit no. 475, prepared by the Japanese War Ministry immediately after the surrender of Japan, and forwarded by them on 19 December 1945 to the Supreme Commander on their own initiative, and not on demand. The Japanese government realised that their credibility as a civilised nation would be put to the test before the eyes of the whole world in the forthcoming International Military Tribunals. The War Ministry knew that many of the alleged war criminals would come from their own ranks, and thus they produced this document which almost amounted to a confession, incorporating any excuses they considered might help their image. To anyone who actually experienced the conditions on the railway this report reads like a fairytale. There are references in it to orders by Imperial General Headquarters, and it was to be part of the prosecution's case that the following accused were members of that body at the material dates: Tōjō, Kimura, Satō on the military side: Shimada, Naganō and Ōka on the naval side. With regard to cruelty directly inflicted on prisoners by individuals, there was no data available

127

in Tokyo. This document was to prove one of the most controversial exhibits introduced by the prosecution and one to which Sir Arthur Comyns Carr so often referred during his direct questioning of Cyril.

MR COMYNS CARR:

Q   'With regard to the statement here that in 1943 Imperial General Headquarters ordered at last to postpone the period of the work by two months, in spite of the fact that this order had a grave influence upon the operations in Burma, what do you say about that?'

Before Cyril could answer, Dr Ichirō Kiyose, for the defence, intervened. Remembered by Arnold Brackman for his white beard and ill-fitting suits, he was an astute and able lawyer who was to be reelected to the Diet (Parliament) in 1952 and become speaker of the house. At this tribunal he was the man who masterminded Tōjō's defence.

DR KIYOSE: 'Mr President, is this an inquiry – is this asking for the witness' opinion?'

THE PRESIDENT (Sir William Webb): 'He is just asking him to make a statement of fact, whether there was any justification for the Japanese claim. Even if it involved giving an opinion, it would be unobjectionable coming from this witness.'

Cyril replied to Sir Arthur's question:

A   'From the time we arrived in our labour camps in May 1943 we were told again and again by the Japanese that the work had to be finished by August. This was quite obviously a physical impossibility because my force alone had thirty miles, approximately, virgin jungle to cut through... From August onwards we were told by the POW Administration that the engineers had lost face because they had not finished the railway on time.'

As pressure intensified the railway engineers were in a permanent rage. The report (exhibit 475) continues saying how difficult it was to raise enough local labour and, as the work was far from the front line, Imperial General Headquarters sanctioned the use of POWs.

Though the Japanese Army did its best in taking the best possible measures conceivable at that time in order to improve the treatment of the prisoners-of-war cooperating with the Japanese troops, laying stress on billeting, ration and health, many prisoners-of-war fell victim of the work at last, much to our regret.

We should like to declare the Japanese troops participated in the joys and sorrows of the prisoners-of-war and native labourers in the construction work, and by no means completed or intended to complete the work only at the sacrifice of prisoners-of-war.

Note: The Director of construction cherished the motto: "Prisoners-of-war and labourers are Fathers of Construction" and consequently endeavoured to improve the treatment of prisoners-of-war.

THE PRESIDENT thought it unnecessary for Colonel Wild to comment.

MR COMYNS CARR:

Q 'Colonel Wild, can you tell us anything about the epidemic prevention and water supply depot?'

A 'I assume that they were units working with the Japanese Army and not prisoners-of-war. I never encountered them.'

Q 'And what about the field hospital of the 21st Division?'

A 'That would be entirely the Japanese. None of our men were in Japanese hospitals.'

Sir Arthur Comyns Carr read again from the Japanese report:

After Major-General Shimoda's death Major-General Takasaki succeeded him as the commander of the railway construction, and arrived at the spot in the middle of February of the same year, and the work was being eagerly carried on as before. Contrary to our expectation, the rainy season set in one April in Thailand and in the middle of April in Burma, which influence upon the work and supply were tremendous.

Q 'Colonel Wild, was it true that the monsoon began earlier than usual in that year?'

A 'I believe it was the usual time, and we warned the Japanese again and again, from information supplied by officers who had been in Burma and Siam before the war, that the monsoon was about to break.'

The report:

At the same time cholera, which had been prevalent in some areas of Burma, was spread over the border-line between Thailand and Burma and, simultaneously with the setting-in of the rainy season, became increasingly prevalent. June was its most prevalent time when there broke out about 6,000 cases (of which 1,200 were the POWs) of which about 4,000 proved fatal (of which about 500 odd were the POWs). Thus many fell victim of the work in a short time. As this fact inspired fear in the labourers on the spot, many fled away and even some cases stole out of a hospital. The situations, dangerous both from the viewpoint of epidemic prevention and the work itself, were brought about.

As cholera was prevailing, the Headquarters not only dispatched medical authorities there, but sent some staff officers in order to make them take necessary steps, and the South Army also often dispatched principal medical officers and some staff officers in order to cope with the situation: the construction units fulfilled their duties, overcoming unfavourable circumstances: the prisoners-of-war earnestly cooperated with them.

Q   'Pausing there: Will you tell me, Colonel Wild, first of all about those figures as to cholera deaths among prisoners-of-war?'

A   'If the figure of 500 fatal cases of cholera refers to June only, I should say it was about correct. If it is meant to be the total figure, it is a great understatement because in F Force alone we lost 700.'

Q   'What about the medical authorities from headquarters and from the Southern Army?'

A   'I recall seeing a Japanese medical major going around one of the camps on one occasion. But that was the only visit he paid to our area.'

Q   'Would this be a suitable point for you to tell us about Dr Woolfe?'

A   'We heard at the Nieke camp at the end of May that about twelve of our men were still at Konkuita camp. Konkuita was the cholera camp which I mentioned earlier, about thirty miles south of us. We therefore got permission from the Japanese to send Assistant-Surgeon Woolfe, an Anglo-Indian, to Konkuita. He found eight of the twelve men in a small tent. Four of them were suffering from cholera. They had had no food or attention from the Japanese for several days and were lying in their own filth. Woolfe paid three visits to the Japanese medical major, whom I have mentioned, whose hut was in that camp. He asked for medical supplies from quite a well-stocked dispensary there. All he was given was some disinfectant to wash his own hands with. He made a strong appeal to this Japanese medical major, saying that the men would die without medical attention. The Japanese major

130

said, "It can't be helped; if they die, they die." Woolfe then tried to move these men to a neighbouring Australian camp. He offered to pay for the transport out of his own money. This was refused. He then carried the men, one by one, and hid them at the side of the road. The Australians were then contacted and recovered the men, whom they took to their camp. I got this report verbally and in writing from Assistant-Surgeon Woolfe immediately he returned from Konkuita.'

Major-General Ishida, the new director of construction, arrived at his post on 16 August 1943. Major-General Takasaki had become ill with malaria at the end of April, 'and yet he continued to fulfil his duty until he fell down on bed.' Sir Arthur Comyns Carr continued his questioning on the conditions pertaining on the railway.

Q   'Colonel Wild, did you ever see Major-General Ishida at the time?'

A   'No, never. He was never in my area or anywhere in my vicinity.'

Q   'Did you come across any trace of an improvement of conditions of the prisoners-of-war between July and October 1943?' (The Japanese report stated that General Ishida had 'renewed the organisation of the staff, endeavoured to stimulate the morale, and was always in the van of the party, the main object of reorganisation being in the innovation and improvement of the supervision of working conditions.')

A   'The worst months from the point of view of treatment and driving of the men were August and September 1943.'

Q   'Colonel Wild, is there really any substance in this suggestion that the Japanese were better suited to meet these hardships than your men?'

A   'I think that was successfully disproved by the Burma Campaign which followed.'

Q   'What do you say about the dress of your men causing them to be exposed to tropical ulcers?'

A   'It is true that the mistake was discovered by the British Army that covering the knees was better than wearing shorts in the jungle, but it is a ridiculous remark here because men were wearing nothing below the knees. They had no boots or shoes or stockings.'

At this point William Logan, Marquis Kidō's defence counsel, interrupted the questioning.

MR LOGAN: 'The defence does not quite understand the purpose of the prosecution in introducing a document, and we assume they vouch for its credibility, and then examining the witness on the stand concerning the document. They are, in effect, anticipating a defence of all the defendants by so doing. This matter should more properly be brought out in rebuttal rather than on direct examination such as this kind.'

MR COMYNS CARR: 'This document is the confession of the Japanese Army with regard to the Burma-Siam railway. It also incorporates such excuses as they could think of. I rely upon the document for the confession. I rely upon this witness to destroy the excuses.'

THE PRESIDENT: 'Objection overruled.'

The Japanese, in this same document, claimed that they gave our doctors instruction on prevention and treatment of malaria.

MR COMYNS CARR:

Q   'What can you say about that list of malaria prevention methods?'

A   'Firstly, it is quite incorrect for the Japanese to suggest that they gave our medical officers any knowledge or training. We had first class medical specialists – tropical medical specialists – among our officers, and the Japanese notion as to tropical hygiene was purely medieval. Eight-man mosquito nets were issued in fairly large quantities to us after we had been in the jungle about two months. They could not be used, as the men were crammed so closely together on the sleeping platforms. There was nothing for the men to sleep on, so the mosquitoes came up through the sleeping platform and the thing became a mosquito trap. There was no preventive oiling of pools whatever and, lastly, it says here that the Japanese were taking prophylactic doses of quinine and plesmohin, but there was never enough to give preventive doses to prisoners-of-war.'

Q   'Have you any comment to make on the figures given?'

A   'In my own force, apart from the three thousand who died, 95% of the survivors had malaria when they came out. The local labourers in our area had a percentage at least as high.'

The report goes on to say that the Japanese made men wear boots and leggings as a precautionary measure against tropical ulcers and, as a remedy, permanganic acid salvarsan was used. In addition, each unit made ointment from lard.

Q   'Pausing there, what do you say about that?'

A   'If we had had lard we should have eaten it.'

MR LOGAN (for the defence) asked to be heard a little further on his objection to the document 475.

THE PRESIDENT: 'I realise that this is not a confession by any of the accused, but the conspiracy is alleged not merely against the accused, but against others as well; and this may be an admission by one of those others. Such an admission may yet be regarded as evidence against all, but the Court has that matter under consideration. It has reserved its decision on that point. Apart altogether from conspiracy, it may be regarded, perhaps, as an admission by some person or persons for whom the accused can hereafter be established as responsible. As it stands it may not, without some connection, be evidence against any of the accused, but we expect that connection to be made later if this is to be used, of course. It would be remarkable if in proceedings like this a document emanating from the Japanese Government could not be used in evidence, subject to the accused being connected with the allegations contained in it. And above all, as you know, we are not bound by the strict rules of evidence, but must receive every document for its probative value; and hearsay is admissible here, and hearsay may be contained in a document as well as in any oral statement. Subject to hearing what you have to say, Mr Logan, it appears to me that only by the strictest adherence to the most technical rules of evidence could we exclude this. Of course, the prosecution has the choice of anticipating the defence and meeting it with evidence in their case in chief, or of waiting to give evidence in rebuttal. They have selected the former course.'

MR LOGAN: 'Well, if the Tribunal please, may I say a few words?'

THE PRESIDENT: 'Yes, I invited you to do so.'

MR LOGAN: 'What we had in mind was this: If the prosecution succeeds in disproving this document, what have they accomplished? Certainly the defence did not introduce this, and we did not expose it to this proof, and it is not a confession of any of these accused, as Your Honour said. The prosecutor said it is a confession of the Government. Now, the Government is not one of the defendants on trial here, and certainly its disapproval cannot be held against any of the accused. In other words, Your Honour, this document was written by the Prisoner-of-War Information Bureau after the war was over. It is not connected with any of these accused and, in effect, it is setting up a straw man for the purpose of knocking him down through this witness. That is what we are objecting to.'

THE PRESIDENT: 'I understand that the objection is not to the evidence actually, which is clearly admissible under the Charter, but to the method which you are employing in examining this man on a document which you rightly tendered. That is the position as I understand it... The objection is overruled.'

Sir Arthur Comyns Carr turned to the subject of food and sanitation during the transportation of prisoners to the railway. He continued to read from the same Japanese document:

As for the supply, the staple food was received from the Army in agreement with the South General Army Intendance Ordinance, the side dishes were served after the menu was drawn up. The actual condition was regularly reported to the Army. The side dishes of fixed quantity were acquired with great pains from all over Thailand, Malay, and French Indo-China and a great effort was made to improve the menu.

Regards to the sanitation during the transportation, an overseer sent from a prisoner camp took charge of it and it was ordered that he would act in concert with medical institutions concerned through a commander of the nearest station. As the actual instances show, the commander paid a special attention to keeping up such prisoner's health as it was on his arrival, and inspected the management of transportation of prisoners at the station, and issued orders carefully about the supply, sanitation and treatment.

Q   'I don't think you will need to say anything more about the side dishes and the menu. You have dealt with those. But about this – about somebody being appointed at the station to look after sanitation during the railway journey?'

A   'I saw no signs of any overseer during transportation by train, as I mentioned earlier. We just used the tracks.'

THE MONITOR: 'What is it, "tracks"?'

THE WITNESS (Cyril): 'Railway tracks.'

THE MONITOR: 'What do you mean by using the tracks?'

THE WITNESS: 'Relieved ourselves on them. The only sanitation provided in the camps was an open trench latrine.'

Typical of this Japanese document is a report on the transportation of POWs by sea, read by Sir Arthur Comyns Carr in Court when it resumed after the weekend break on *Monday 16 September 1946.*

The equipments for transportation of personnel are as follows:

1. Setting aside indispensable vessels, all were two-storied. Still further in every spare room on the decks, two or three-storied berths were equipped as it was called the "Decisive battle transportation". Thus the capacity was increased.

2. The space between the upper and the lower stories was regulated not to touch the head in sitting attitude (about 0.75 metre in minimum).

3. As the capacity was increased as far as possible, with an equipment of such berths as said in 1 and 2, each person lost the freedom of his action in a ship when the ship was damaged by a torpedo and many persons and munitions were sunk to the bottoms of the sea.

This caused the greatest difficulty in the operation of the Japanese army and its fighting power of long duration. About this matter, it is supposed that your navy knows well.

The bad ventilation and the bad and inconstant supply and the loss of sleep (it was impossible to lie down) due to the closest packing caused the conspicuous increase of patients during the transportation. Even those who did not fall ill during the transportations must be at rest for a time after landing, or else they sometimes became unable to fight a severe battle.

For that reason the shipping space was calculated to economise as far as possible, the water-closet being put outside gunnel... It is desired that you acknowledge the war-prisoners were not closely packed up only because they were war-prisoners. That they were kept from coming out on the decks may be from the viewpoint of guarding and preventing of espionage of the voyage of ship groups.

It may be supposed that the war-prisoners transported to the Thailand-Burma Railway area were treated better than in any other areas.

Q   'Pausing there, Colonel Wild, do you see any reason for that supposition, as far as your information goes?'

A   'I should just like to explain that the system whereby prisoners were carried to Siam was the same as in other voyages. The

135

system, in fact, was that wooden stages were built up in empty coal bunkers and in holds with three-foot clearance between one stage and the next one. Where it says that 29 men were carried in the space of one cubic "*tsubo*", that means that 14 to 15 men sat cross-legged on these planks in an area six feet by six feet; and three feet above their heads another 14 or 15 men were sitting in the same space, and so on to the top of the hold or the bunkers. Where this was harder on the prisoners than on Japanese was because their average height was greater, and they were not accustomed to sitting cross-legged. Also, they were usually suffering from dysentery – had some cases of dysentery among them when they embarked – and they were not allowed on deck during the voyage. This applied to the voyages to Siam or Burma as well as to other voyages, and I know that one Dutch ship going from NEI to that destination had extremely heavy casualties during the voyage.'

Q   'About the suggestion that not allowing them on deck was a precaution against espionage, what do you say?'

A   'That is a good instance of the age-old Japanese preoccupation with espionage, and it is difficult to see what possible use the prisoners could have made of the information if they had obtained it.'

Q   'If they were unable to transport the prisoners under proper conditions, was there any necessity for transporting them at all?'

MR LOGAN: 'If the Tribunal please – '

THE PRESIDENT: 'Mr Logan.'

MR LOGAN: 'We object to that question. We think it is purely argumentative and not to be decided by this witness.'

THE PRESIDENT: 'It is a question an expert might answer, and he is an expert.'

A   'No doubt the Japanese considered it necessary but what, as prisoners, we were stressing to them again and again was that they had not the right to move prisoners unless they had proper means to do so, nor the right to detain them in places like the Siam jungle where they were unable to feed and supply them.'

The Japanese report 475 continued by saying that it was the lack of means of transport that forced men to march on foot to their camps on the railway, but 'at every 20 or 25 kms along the march line a pavilion (camping by means of tent) was set up, with a tea-supplying place in the interval. A great effort was made to check epidemics on the marching road, and stragglers were taken to the nearest sanitary institution. For this means motor cars were driven along in order to make liaison and to take stragglers in.'

Q   'Now, Colonel Wild, you have given us your account of this matter; is there any particular additional comment you want to make on this account of it?'

A   'The so-called pavilion which was set up at every twenty or twenty-five kilometres meant, in effect, the accommodation which was provided for the Japanese. After the beating which Major Hunt and I had sustained at Tarsao we did, in a sense, win our battle to the extent of being allowed to put, say, thirty sick in the POW hospital at Tarsao.[5] We did see Japanese infantry marching up the road and they were not having an easy time. I said myself, earlier, that as an infantry soldier I consider it would have been an arduous march for fit troops. The Japanese were fit and well fed. We were half-starved and had two thousand non-walking sick to push along. As regards the rest days, the last march of the British troops who went to Sonkurai camp were five successive night stages in the worst of the monsoon rains, and they were taken out to work the next day.'

This lengthy report, made by the Japanese Government on the Burma-Siam Railway in December 1945, on which Cyril had now been examined for several days, concludes:

1. The foregoing is an explanation of the circumstances which compelled a heavy toll of life during the progress of the construction work. In the final analysis, causes of the tragedy may be traced principally to the placement of a time limit on the construction, the immense difficulty in making thorough preparation and to the precipitancy with which the Japanese soldiers, despite their lack of experience in such large-scale construction work and meagre scientific equipment, dared to carry on their work in strict obedience to orders which they characteristically regarded as imperative. Thus the occurrence of the casualties, it must be declared, was by no means due to any deliberate intention on the part of the Army authorities.

As regards the employment of prisoners-of-war in the above construction work, it may be stated that at the time the Japanese Army as a whole entertained the ideas that the employment of prisoners-of-war, in any work other than military operations, was not a breach of the Geneva Convention. Furthermore, it is to be insisted that the incident was of a radically different character from the so-called maltreatment of prisoners-of-war.

2. The incident, already stated, was an inevitable outcome of the situation then prevailing and, if anyone is to be called to account for the dreadful death rate, the responsibility ought to be placed on the then Chief of the General Staff (General Sugiyama) who ordered the construction,[6] the War Minister (General Tōjō) who sanctioned the employment of prisoners, and the Commander-in-Chief of the South Area Corps (General Terauchi) who was entrusted with the construction on the spot.

As regards individual cases of maltreatment of prisoners-of-war, it is desired that investigation be started upon the further receipt from the Allied Powers of a report of the details, particularly the ranks and names of the suspected offenders and if, as a result, they should be found guilty severe measures should be meted out to them.

Q   'Now Colonel Wild, while you have been in Tokyo have you made some further investigations?'

A   'Yes, I have, particularly in Sugamo Prison.'

Q   'And has it come to light that there is in existence a complete series of reports by this War Ministry Committee, dealing with prisoners-of-war over all the Pacific area?'

A   'Yes, as a result of my interrogations 26 more documents have come to light, similar to the one which you have been reading.'

Sugamo Prison, a grim collection of square ugly buildings containing 700 cells, was where those Japanese arrested as potential war criminals were held. The area of the prison covered four acres and accommodated 1,073 inmates and 365 guards.

After indictment the 28 defendants being tried at Ichigaya were returned to their individual cells each evening. The doors of the cells had been removed and a guard was posted in front of each one. It was necessary that they were watched closely to prevent them committing *hara kiri*, and indeed several objects that could have been used for this purpose were removed from them. A *haramake*, a six-foot sash used by Japanese soldiers as an athletic supporter, was taken from General Tōjō as it was thought he could have hanged himself with it; a piece of steel wire, sharpened on a wall, was found in General Itagaki's cell; a pair of false-bottomed shoes was found on Toshiō Shiratori; and a pair of chopsticks shaved into stilettos was removed from the cell of Admiral Nagano – the man who had approved the exact timing for the attack on Pearl Harbour.

Former Premier Hideki Tōjō had already tried to commit suicide by shooting himself as the US military police moved in to arrest him as a war criminal on 11 September 1945. He was rushed to hospital in time.

The next discussion centred on Document Nᵒ· 2647, exhibit Nᵒ· 476. This report was drawn up in October 1945 by a 'Prisoner-of-War Investigation Committee' on the orders of Lieutenant-General Shimomura, Minister of War, and chaired by Lieutenant-General Waka-matsu, Vice-Minister of War. Other members were Lt-Col Oishi (chief of the *Kempeitai* in Singapore), Lt-Col Hashizume, Lt-Col Kinotake and Lt-Col Fujiwara.

A sub-committee was formed, chaired by Colonel Sugita, on what the Japanese themselves called the 'Chinese Massacre' in Singapore. Sugita was under direct orders of Wakamatsu.

The report by the sub-committee claimed that during the two to three day gap between the day of the British surrender and the day of the Japanese entry into the city the Chinese had been looting and storing for future use 'implements of war'. To this, Cyril stated quite emphatically that there had been no such gap, as Japanese troops were already on duty in Singapore when he left Fort Canning at 8 o'clock in the morning on 16 February 1942 to go to another conference with Colonel Sugita at Bukit Timah.

MR COMYNS CARR:

Q 'Now, during all the time that you had been in Malaya before the Japanese invasion, had there been disturbances? Was the population given to disturbances?'

A 'Certainly not. Malaya was a very happy place in my observation, and the happiest thing about it was the way in which Indians, Malays and Chinese, many races, lived in peace with one another.'

The report admits that 5,000 Chinese were punished strictly up to the end of March 1942.

Q 'Colonel Wild, I noticed the expression, "punished strictly", in the last line that I read before the adjournment. Is that one with which you became familiar in captivity?'

139

A   'Yes, we learned in captivity that that was the accepted Japanese euphemism for execution.'

The sub-committee further reported:

> The 5th and 18th Division commenced the subjugation operation from nearly the beginning of March, carrying out research and subjugation of anti-Japan Chinese in cities and jungles and we caught wicked Chinese till the end of April.

Cyril, in his testimony, recounted how at this time a whole Eurasian settlement near Johore city – men, women and children – were murdered and, on the evidence of witnesses, the bodies had been exhumed just before he flew up to Tokyo.

The report continued:

> ... Although it is not possible to guarantee that, in making the arrests and punishments, the staff officers concerned did not ''overdo'' themselves, and although it is difficult to get a clear idea of the situation then because Lt-Col Hayashi, who was the staff officer in charge of it (staff officer attached to the headquarters of the *Shōnan* Garrison Forces[7]), and Chief-of-Staff Lieutenant-General Suzuki have died in action, it may become further clear if Major-General Iketani, who was the chief of the operations section, and Colonel Tsūji who was the staff officer in charge of operations, are interrogated.

Q   'Colonel Wild, have you been able to find either of those gentlemen?'

A   'I know where they are.'

Later:

Q   'Now, there are just two short matters I want to ask you about further, Colonel Wild. One is this: Did you, while in captivity, get to know of any protests that were being made by the British Government about your treatment?'

A   'Yes, we did.'

Q   'In particular, do you remember the speech by Mr Eden coming through?'

A   'I read the full text of Mr Eden's protest regarding the Burma-Siam Railway in Changi camp the day after it had been delivered.'

Q   'Do you remember the date, approximately?'

A   'I would say January 1944. It made a great impression on us at the time as we had left Siam only a few weeks before, and it read like the statement of an eye witness.'

The Times Weekly Edition of Wednesday 22 November 1944 reports that the Secretary of State for War, Sir James Grigg, made a statement to the House of Commons on the previous Friday, confirming the conditions under which prisoners-of-war were held. The information had been gathered from 60 British survivors among the 152 prisoners-of-war rescued by United States naval forces after a Japanese transport had been sunk in transit from Singapore to Japan. The only redeeming feature, Sir James Grigg commented, was the amazing morale of all prisoners.

After a short 15 minute recess the Tribunal resumed and Sir Arthur Comyns Carr continued his questioning of Cyril:

Q   'How did you get the information through in the prison camps that you have been telling us about?'

A   'In every camp I was in we always had our secret wireless receivers with which we used to listen in to the BBC, New Delhi, Australia, Chungking, and San Francisco.'

Q   'Did the Japanese ever discover them?'

A   'I remember their discovery of one at Kanburi within a day or so of my arrival there from the jungle.'

Q   'What did they do to the people concerned?'

A   'They were six British officers; three of them had been concerned in it and three had not been concerned in it, although they lived in the same hut. Under the directions of the Japanese camp commandant, these six British officers were flogged with heavy sticks for four hours, between about one o'clock in the morning and about five o'clock in the morning. Two of them died after about two and a half hours' flogging. The case was one of the first to be tried in Singapore, and the Japanese officer and his chief assistants were hanged. The remainder were sentenced to long terms of imprisonment.'

These officers were arrested in Kanchanaburi in September 1943. The two who died were Capt. Jack Hawley, RASC, and Lieutenant Armitage, RA. The four survivors were Major W.G. Smith, who was 50 years old at the time, Major Jim Slater, RA, who died at a young age soon after the war, Morton Mackay, A Canadian, and Lieutenant Eric Lomax, 9th Indian Division, Signals, whose arms were broken during the flogging. They were court-martialled in Bangkok before being brought down to Outram Road Gaol on 30 November 1943.

The timing of this particular radio episode may have contributed to the 'Double Tenth' barbarity (See Pages 50 & 109). Cyril and Eric Lomax had met on a previous occasion early in their captivity, at Changi camp in 1942 (See page 38).

Q   'Since you have been engaged in war crimes investigation in South-East Asia Command, approximately how many cases have been brought to trial there?'

A   'Over three hundred by now; including those undergoing trial, nearly four hundred.'

Q   'And with what results, again broadly stated?'

A   'Well over a hundred death sentences and about a hundred and fifty terms of imprisonment.'

Q   'Have some been acquitted?'

A   'About fifty.'

Q   'Now, is that exclusive of those brought to trial by Australian courts, Dutch courts and American courts?'

A   'Exclusive, except that some of the Dutch, American, and so on, cases have been tried in Singapore; but excluding a large number tried in areas outside Singapore.'

MR COMYNS CARR: 'That is all I have to ask the witness.'

THE PRESIDENT: 'Mr Blewett.'

MR BLEWETT (for the defence): 'If Your Honours please, this witness has travelled a long and circuitous road covering a vast territory – '

THE PRESIDENT: 'Now, you must examine him and not give us a sermon on his evidence.'

MR BLEWETT: 'If Your Honour please, I am – '

THE PRESIDENT: 'No preliminary statements, Mr Blewett. Proceed with your cross-examination.'

George F. Blewett was Tōjō's Philadelphia lawyer, working with Dr Ichirō Kiyose on his defence. With his Japanese colleague, Mr Shiohara, he proceeded to cross-question Cyril for two days, mainly concerning the signatures on the document, exhibit 475, and on the sources of the information given in Cyril's testimony. This interminable labouring on fine details is illustrative of the drawn-out rhetoric on the part of several defence lawyers. The defence, both Japanese and American, was often deliberately obstructive.

Mr Blewett then questioned Cyril on his duties as liaison officer during his week at Fort Canning immediately following the Allied surrender, on the opportunities he had of escape at that time, and on whether he received preferential treatment because of his language ability. On this latter point Cyril was indignant:

A   'Throughout the whole of my captivity I took a pride in having exactly the same treatment as any of my men. I should be ashamed now if I could think of one instance where I had received preferential treatment from the Japanese. And that applies to the Burma-Siam Railway as much as to Singapore Island.'[8]

Mr Blewett found he was quite unable to destroy any of Cyril's testimony and, on *Wednesday 18 September*, admitted that he had been mistaken in a reference he had made to General Percival's wife, and that he was referring to the wife of another senior officer.

Thursday 19 September

MR COMYNS CARR (reexamining Cyril):

Q   'Now the last matter: You were asked about courtesies extended to the wife of a general officer, or to a general officer as the result of the illness of his wife. First it was suggested that it was General Percival, and then that it was some other officer. I think you must tell us the real facts about that, please. Colonel Wild.'

A   'The lady in question was Lady Heath, the wife of my own Corps Commander. She was a very brave woman. I've seen her under shellfire. She refused to leave Singapore while it was besieged or before. She was doing some welfare work, and I think that both she and perhaps the Corps Commander too hoped that, if they survived the fall of the city, the Japanese might leave them together.'

Q   'Where was she placed after the fall of the city?'

143

A   'In Changi Gaol. The General was in Changi camp.'

Q   'Did you succeed in obtaining any interviews with her while she was in the gaol?'

A   'Yes, I did. She was the lady I mentioned having seen twice in Changi Gaol.'

Q   'What was her state of health?'

A   'When I saw her she was partially recovered from a very dangerous illness.'

Q   'Had she been in Changi Gaol all the time?'

A   'No, she was sent to the hospital in about June or July 1942 where she gave birth to a child. The child was dead and, in the opinion of the gynaecologist, his life would have been saved if two pots of marmite had been given to her shortly before the birth.'

Q   'Had she been adequately fed in Changi Gaol?'

A   'Not in the way in which I would have expected somebody in her condition to be looked after.'[9]

Q   'After your release did you see Sir Lewis and Lady Heath again?'

A   'Yes, I did, but I saw him as well just after this episode had taken place at Changi.'

Q   'What was his own state of health at that time?'

A   'He was suffering from amoebic dysentery, and he was none the better for the treatment which he had had in Fort Canning, as I described previously, from Major Hayashi.'[10]

Q   'Later was he sent out of Malaya?'

A   'Yes. He missed the boat with the other general officers, on account of his illness, and he went to Formosa later in the year, in October or November.'

Q   'And where did his wife remain?'

A   'She remained in the hospital for some time and then she was put in a convent for a little while during her illness, and then returned to Changi Prison. She was back in Changi Prison certainly by the beginning of 1943.'

Q   'Now, did you see them both after the war, after your release?'

A   'Yes, I did.'

Q   'Did he show you anything at that time, or was it at the earlier time you saw him that he showed you a document?'

A   'It was on the earlier occasion, in August 1942, that he showed me a newspaper.'

Q   'Yes. What newspaper was it?'

A   'It was the official Japanese propaganda newspaper in English called the *Singapore Shimbun*.'

Q   'What particular part of the newspaper did he show you?'

A   'He showed me an item at the left of the page, about two-thirds of a column long. I remember the look of it to this day.'

Q   'What did it purport to be?'

A   'It purported to be a letter of thanks from General Heath to the commander of the Japanese forces. It was couched in the most fulsome terms remarking, among other things, that no other nation in the world could have matched the *bushidō* of the Japanese Army in the treatment which they had given to Lady Heath.'

Q   'And what did General Heath say about that letter?'

A   'He mentioned first what he thought about the way she had, in fact, been treated. Then he pointed at this passage and said to me, "I have learned a good deal about Japanese *bushidō*[11] during the last few months. This is a bare-faced forgery and I could not have believed that any army in the world would have stooped to such baseness."'

MR COMYNS CARR: 'That is all I have to ask the witness, Your Honour.'

THE PRESIDENT: 'The witness may go on the usual terms.

Cyril finished his testimony at the Tokyo Major War Crimes Tribunal on Thursday 19 September 1946. When the Tribunal finally concluded on 10 April 1948, twenty-five out of the original twenty-eight defendants were sentenced. Yosuke Matsuoka and Admiral Osami Naganō died of natural causes before judgment was delivered, and Shumei Ōkawa had gone mad. Seven were sentenced to death, and the remaining eighteen were given terms of imprisonment ranging from seven years to life. Mamoru Shigemitsu, one-time Foreign Minister, received the shortest sentence. Dr Ichirō Kiyose, Deputy Chief of the Japanese Defence Section, was said to have been masterful on behalf of Tōjō, and to have won the admiration of all who followed the progress of the Trial. Sir William Webb finally read the judgment in November 1948, two and a half years after the Tribunal was convened in April 1946. The seven defendants sentenced to death were: Doihara, Hirota, Itagaki, Kimura, Matsui, Mutō and Tōjō. Those sentenced to life imprisonment were all paroled in 1954/55.

An article in *The Times* after the conclusion of the tribunal, headed 'Tokyo War Guilt Trial', closed with this paragraph:

> But if the trial has not convinced the Japanese people of their war guilt, it has at least achieved one thing. It has revealed to them their country's record of deceit, treachery, and aggression during the past 20 years. The horrors of the rape of Nanking, the secret pacts with Germany, the exploitation of the Netherlands East Indies, the encouragement of traffic in narcotics, the ruthless consumption of the lives of Allied prisoners-of-war, as related in the sober testimony of the late Colonel C.H.D. Wild, on the Burma-Siam railway – all these things, long concealed by a rigorous censorship, the Tribunal has at last made known to the people of Japan.

Cyril's next assignment was in Singapore. In August 1946 he had written to David: 'I cannot come home for a month or two, as two of my biggest cases are coming up for trial in August – my own F Force (Burma-Siam Railway) and Outram Road Gaol (the "Little Belsen of the East"), for which I did all 65 of the arrests myself in Johore last October. I only missed one of the men I wanted: he was the executioner, who very sensibly executed himself just before I got him. I hope to fly up to Japan between these two cases, as I should like to see what is left of the old place before I leave.'

As we know Cyril did, of course, fly to Japan for the War Crimes Tribunal in Tokyo, but this was *before* his two big cases came up for trial in Singapore. At that time it was not easy to get a seat on any flight between Tokyo and Singapore, but he managed to reach Hong Kong where he remained stranded, together with his colleague, Mr Spencer Davies of the Judge Advocate's Department, also involved in the Tokyo trials.

On the evening of 24 September they dined at Victoria Barracks with Colonel J.F. Crossley, MBE, and Jack Edwards, MBE, both members of the administrative teams for war crimes in Hong Kong, Taiwan and Shanghai. Their coffee was interrupted by the arrival of an orderly with an urgent message for Cyril and Mr Davies. Two civilian passengers had been taken off the passenger list of the RAF Dakota due to leave at 09.30 next morning, and seats were available for them. Cyril was delighted, he could now rejoin Celia and continue with his work in Singapore.

At 09.39 on 25 September the Dakota, with 14 passengers and five crew, took off from Kai Tak airport in the direction of Kowloon Tong, wobbled in the air – and disappeared. The wreckage was found on the lower slopes of a hill between Lion Rock and Beacon Hill. There were no survivors. Cyril was 38.

One of the sadder aspects of this tragic accident was the way in which Celia learnt of Cyril's death. The first she knew of it was when she read the headlines in the Singapore evening paper. Poor Celia. They had come through separation, uncertainties, hardships and shortages of war, and should have been able to look forward to happy and more settled times together. Now she was completely alone and far from home.

Cyril had worked relentlessly for almost a year after the Japanese surrender to bring to justice any alleged war criminal brought to his notice. Near the end of his work as Liaison Officer he said that almost his greatest pleasure was 'letting the little brutes out and sending them off home, and so perhaps it was time to stop'.

Cyril's untimely death was a tragedy. He was a unique man of his time, with great patriotic fervour and a high moral code. He would never allow criticism of his country, his regiment or, in particular, the men who served under him. He was loyal. Those of us who knew him are privileged, and the families of those who did not return must draw some comfort from his relentless and exacting search to bring before the courts those responsible for their losses. He was a brilliant and caring person, with so much to give.

NOTES

[1] See page 42 and 49

[2] See page 53

[3] The author's escape attempt.

[4] Lieutenant Ian Moffat, RE.

[5] see page 47

[6] Sugiyama shot himself after Emperor Hirohito's surrender broadcast.

[7] *Shōnan*: Light of the South, Japanese name for Singapore.

[8] See page 38

[9] See page 107

[10] This refers to the 48 hours when General Heath was incarcerated in a room in Fort Canning without water or food. See page 39.

[11] *bushidō* – the way of the warrior, medieval concept revived in the early 1800s, and developed by the Army in the 1930s in their militaristic propaganda.

EPILOGUE

What an irony of fate that Cyril's principal War Crimes Trial, 'F Force, Burma-Siam Railway', was due to start in Singapore on 26 September, within 24 hours of his death. The work in bringing the alleged criminals to trial had taken months to complete, and he had covered great distances. The whole case was very near to his heart. He knew both the defendants and the witnesses personally and, above all, had lived through those hard and cruel times himself. Like everyone, he had not come through the ordeal unscathed, but he will always be remembered by those of us who were there with the greatest respect and affection.

Cyril was awarded the MBE, Military Division, for his outstanding work with F Force. This, I believe, is the highest award that can be made to a prisoner-of-war.

In view of Cyril's close association with the F Force trial I feel that a brief account must be given here. His evidence was, of course, incorporated as sworn statements which he had made earlier when preparing the case for the prosecution for the Legal Department.

The Court was convened by GOC Singapore at the Supreme Court in Singapore on 26 September 1946 and continued until 23 October. The President was Lt-Col E. N. Blacklock, King's Own Scottish Borderers, and the Prosecuting Counsel were Mr J. St J. Eber, Inner Temple, and Captain Dixon, Australian Army Legal Corps. The accused were:

Lt Hiroshi Ābe   Capt. Hajime Maruyama
Lt-Col Hirateru Banno   Capt. (Medical) Susuma Taniō
Capt. Tsuneō Fukuda   Civilian Kisel Tōyōyama
Civilian Eishin Ishimoto

and the charge was: Violation of the laws and usages of war when engaged in the administration of a group of British and Australian Prisoners-of-War, known as F Force, in construction of the Burma-Siam railway and were together concerned in the inhumane treatment of the said POWs, resulting in the deaths of many and in the physical suffering of many of the other said prisoners-of-war.

Lt-Col Banno, on the orders of General Arimura, had assumed command of F Force on 10May 1943, and established his HQ at Nieke. During the trial Banno, in answer to the question: 'On whose order was the construction started?', said, 'I heard a proposal was made by Southern Force HQ to the General Staff Board of the Imperial Japanese Army, Tokyo, and the order was issued by Marshal-General Sugiyama, who was head of the General Staff. I consider Sugiyama responsible.' (He may, or may not, have known that General Hajime Sugiyama had already committed suicide after Emperor Hirohito's surrender broadcast. See page 117)

Cyril had said earlier that the building of the railway was one of the 'horrors of war' and, in his written testimony, he stated that Sonkurai was the worst camp of all, under the command of an NCO, Corporal Gotō, with fifteen Korean guards. I like to think that our escape achieved something for those we left behind at Sonkurai because, as a result of it, Corporal Gotō was sacked and was replaced by Lieutenant Wakabayashi. This man proved to be one of the most reasonable of any Japanese in charge of a camp, and Cyril refers to him in his report on F Force.[1] When Lt-Col Dillon and Cyril were sent up to Sonkurai from Nieke at the end of August 1943, Dillon was able to pull the camp round in two months with the cooperation of Lieutenant Wakabayashi, but Lieutenant Hiroshi Ābe, the engineer in charge of construction, was conspicuous at all times in failing to stop brutal treatment by his men, even in his presence.

Capt. Fukuda, at his trial, addressed the Court from the dock: 'At the beginning of my statement I like to express my sincere regret and sorrow for those who died in the construction of the railway. I would also like to express my appreciation for the work the POWs presented and especially Colonel Wild, Major Hunt and Major Stevens.'

Maruyama, Fukuda, Tōyōyama and Ābe were sentenced to death. Taniō was given five years, Banno three years, and Ishimoto 18 months. The sentences were confirmed by GOC Singapore, Major-General Cox, on 7 January 1947. Those of Maruyama and Ābe were commuted to 15 years, and those of Fukuda and Tōyōyama were commuted to life.

Cyril had also investigated another group of senior officers in connection with their activities and responsibilities on the Burma-Siam railway. They came up for trial in Singapore in October 1946, with the trial lasting until December, the President of the Tribunal being Lt-Col P. A. Forsythe, MM, King's Royal Rifle Corps. Colonel Shigeo Nakamura, in command of the Siam POW administration from 20 June 1943 to 24 July 1944, whose HQ was Kanchanaburi, was found to have failed in his responsibility for the well-being of prisoners-of-war. He was sentenced to death on 3 December 1946, and this was confirmed by Major-General Cox on 25 March 1947. He was hanged in Changi Gaol on 26 March 1947, as also was Colonel Tamie Ishii. The other three defendants in this case received sentences ranging from 10 to 20 years.

Cyril's other big case, for which he had worked so assiduously and had made the arrests himself, was the trial of the Commandant of Outram Road Gaol, Singapore, Capt. Koshirō Mikizawa, and his assistant, Takeshi Nōda. Others concerned in this case were tried on a separate occasion.[2]

The Military Court for the Trial of War Criminals was convened by GOC Singapore District on 14 November 1946 and ended on 22 December 1946. The President was Lt-Col R. L. Le Gallais, Dept of Judge Advocate-General in India. The defendant, Capt. Koshirō Mikizawa, who was attached to the IJA, was charged with: 'Committing a war crime in that at Singapore between 1 November 1943 and 15 August 1945, when responsible for the well-being of prisoners in custody in the civil section of the Outram Road Prison, were in violation of the laws and usages of war, together concerned as parties to the ill-treatment and neglect of certain of such prisoners causing the death of about one thousand prisoners and physical suffering of other prisoners there in custody.'

As a civilian before the war Mikizawa's occupation had been as a judicial official. Now it was revealed that, between those two dates when he was in charge of the gaol as Governor, 1,283 deaths occurred, and the total number of bodies removed by disposal of the dead was 1,113. On one occasion Mikizawa was heard to have said to a prisoner-of-war, 'If the prisoners die, never mind.'

During his trial Mikizawa stated: 'I think that, judged by the standard of prisons in Japan, the conditions in Outram Road Gaol were in no way inferior. Most died of beri-beri and dysentery. My feelings towards the prisoners were the same as towards my children, and I always forbade the guards to beat the prisoners.'

Mikizawa's plea was: Not guilty. The finding was: Guilty. On 22 December 1946 he was sentenced to life imprisonment, and his civilian assistant, Takeshi Nōda, was sentenced to five years.

These last trials in Singapore, which Cyril had always considered would be his major ones, were the culmination of his work as War Crimes Liaison Officer. Had he lived, I believe he would have returned home satisfied that justice had been done, although he was in no way vindictive. I also believe that he would have been ready to forgive, to put the past behind him and look to the future – but *never* to forget.

Cyril Wild's grave is in the Happy Valley Cemetery, Hong Kong. The inscription on the headstone reads:

COLONEL C.H.D. WILD, MBE
THE OXFORDSHIRE AND
BUCKINGHAMSHIRE LIGHT INF.
25TH SEPTEMBER 1946 AGE 38

Canon James Mansel, KCVO, whose late wife, Ann, was Celia's sister, writes: 'Cyril and Celia were vivid and unforgettable personalities, and I am glad you are thinking of a record of a man of unusual gifts and charm, who would have had a notable contribution to make to life if he had survived.'

After Cyril's death Celia returned to England and lived in Winchester, near Ann and James, until she died in 1959.

Cyril's three brothers, the Very Reverend John Wild, the Reverend Patrick Wild and the Reverend David Wild, continued in their ministries. Patrick died in October 1983. John and Margaret, and David and Mary now live in retirement in Somerset.

NOTES

[1] See pages 48 and 53

[2] Cyril's evidence on Outram Road Gaol in the Tokyo trials, page 120

APPENDIX I
AWARD

Recommendation for Award
Major C.H.D. Wild, Oxf. & Bucks. Lt Infty.
GSO2 III Indian Corps.

Major C.H.D. Wild was attached to F Force Headquarters as an additional staff officer and senior interpreter. To Headquarters he was invaluable in suggesting methods of presenting problems to the Japanese. He displayed a deep insight into their character and a thorough understanding of their mental processes and likely reactions. On at least two occasions it was his own resolution and capacity to seize opportunities that resulted in some immediate and permanent amelioration in the lot of the whole force. As interpreter in local camp work his duties involved him in every unpleasant incident which occurred and here he showed the highest resolution and courage, which on many occasions led to the removal of difficulties and sometimes to the punishment or repression of bullies amongst our guards. On one occasion his efforts to prevent sick men being made to march led to his being savagely beaten himself.

At all times throughout the eight months in Thailand this officer was conspicuous for his imperturbable courage, his intelligence and resource in handling the Japanese and his wholehearted loyalty to his commanders.

His conduct was an inspiration and example to all ranks.

signed: S.W. Harris, Lt-Col, RA

drafted by Lt-Col F.J. Dillon, MC, AA & QMG, 18th Div.)

APPENDIX II
TRIBUTES

Letter to The Very Revd John Wild from Lt-Gen. A.E. Percival:

29 September 1946

Dear Wild,

Although we have never met, I want to write and send you my very real sympathy on the tragic death of your brother at Hong Kong. It came as a great shock to me and, I am sure also, to the very wide circle of friends he had in the Far East. It is not for me to tell you of his exceptional qualities – you no doubt know them better than I do – but I can tell you something of the wonderful work he did in Malaya and Siam both before and during the period of captivity.

I first got to know him as a Staff Officer on the Headquarters 3rd Indian Corps, where I formed a very high opinion of his ability – as I know his immediate commander, General Heath, did also.

But his best work was done during the period of captivity. He had a responsible position at this time as officer interpreter and he was tireless in his work for his fellow prisoners. He showed great courage in the way he stood up to the Japanese – which was no easy matter in those conditions – and won universal admiration and esteem. I was so glad when he was rewarded with an MBE for which I among others recommended him.

As you may know, Cyril was a personal friend of mine – partly because I have known your Uncle Wilfrid for a very long time – and I always had a great admiration for him. I still have a vivid recollection of the last occasion I met him, when he lunched with me early this year. He was so full of the joy of life and kept me interested and amused for a long time. It is a memory that will long remain with me.

I have today written a short appreciation which I have sent to *The Times*. I hope they will publish it.

With kind regards,

Yours sincerely,

signed: A. E. Percival
(Lt-Gen., formerly GOC Malaya)

154

Obituary written by Lieutenant-General A. E. Percival, which appeared in *The Times* in September 1946:

I write on behalf of all who served in Malaya in 1941 – 42 and who afterwards experienced the rigours of three and a half years of captivity in Japanese hands, to express our heartfelt sorrow at the tragic death of Cyril Wild in an air accident at Hong Kong on 25 September 1946.

Before the war Wild was in business in Japan, where, in addition to becoming a fluent Japanese speaker, he acquired a wide knowledge of the characteristics and mentality of the Japanese. In 1941 he became a valuable member of the General Staff of the 3rd Indian Corps in Malaya. His sound judgment, ability, and enthusiasm marked him out as an officer of great promise. It was, however, during the period of captivity that he found the greatest scope for his talents. As interpreter he fought for the interests of his fellow prisoners with unflinching and never failing courage. There were few, either on Singapore Island or in those camps in Siam where he was stationed, who did not at some time or other benefit directly or indirectly from his efforts. After the war he continued his work by accepting an appointment as War Crimes Liaison Officer under the South-East Asia Command, in which capacity he was still serving at the time of his death.

The following extracts are taken from letters to John Wild from two of Cyril's fellow prisoners-of-war:

He was one of the outstanding personalities of our community and, of all those who have ever permitted me some degree of their friendship, he was one of the men I admired and respected most.

After my return to England I was delighted to hear that the authorities had given him the high rank and position for which his combination of courage, personality and judgment fitted him so magnificently, and I know that feeling was shared by many others who had similarly benefited from his exertions while we were prisoners-of-war.

I saw him last, for a brief passing greeting, just after Lord Louis Mountbatten had hoisted the famous flag from Fort Canning at the Singapore Victory Parade.

No-one that I knew in those years deserved more richly a happy and prosperous future and, though we were never together for an extended period of time, his passing gives me a great feeling of personal loss.

R. Scott Russell

– – –

... Physically I was in pretty rotten shape and, in this direction, Cyril literally looked after me, not allowing me to do more than he thought I ought. I got on my feet again largely due to the way he helped me to do it, and then when I started with my pen he became interested at once. Earlier attempts of mine he took and read, ploughing through my appalling writing, offering me the soundest possible advice and keeping me at my new efforts. All this in spite of the fact that he was senior interpreter, and much more than that, to a camp of 50,000 men.

When we first met as prisoners in the room which we shared Wild sat down and almost immediately said, "There are three things that should be done in this camp before I leave it." As you can imagine, he got them done. I remember, too, when the Japanese ordered him to appear in a film of the fall of Singapore. I came back from a job to find him standing in the garden we cultivated ourselves. He told me he wanted to talk to me and then, after telling me what was suggested, he said, "They can shoot me if they like. I won't."

Things were always as simple as that with him. He was quite incapable of any of that compromise which seemed to seep into our life and become one of the worst aspects of being a POW. Cyril never stood down. The result was, of course, that the Japanese both feared and respected him, and he was of more use to his fellow prisoners than all the elaborate "policies" of a hundred senior officers.

Speaking for myself, I know certainly that anything I may have been able to do later on in Japan was due to the lead which Cyril gave me in the time we were together...

It seems petty and mean to tie a feeling of loss to one's own desire for continued support and encouragement. But Cyril kept me going when probably no-one else would have bothered. My affection came from those very human roots. At one time he led me into living again. That is how I feel his death.

Oswald Morris Wynd

N.B. Oswald Wynd is the author of *The Ginger Tree*, which was recently made into a successful television serial.

APPENDIX III

THE FLAG

On the eve of his flight to London to attend the Victory Parade, his office of Supreme Allied Commander South-East Asia having come to an end, Admiral Lord Louis Mountbatten took part in a final ceremony in May 1946, when the Union Jack was formally presented to the city of Singapore. Cyril wrote on 15 May to David:

> I have a fearsome job ahead of me on 29 May, as I have to present the old Union Jack to the Governor at a formal parade, which will also be the Supremo's farewell appearance. It is then handed back to me and I process with it into the Municipal Building, accompanied by my escort of two Cameronian officers and followed by HE, the Supremo, their gilded staffs and all the city fathers. It is then to be hung up in the Council Chamber where I saw the Japs surrender.

The Council Chamber of the Municipal Buildings, therefore, was the last known resting place of the Union Jack. Several years later reports appeared in national newspapers to the effect that it had been removed from the Council Chamber, and this prompted David to write to Admiral Lord Mountbatten. The latter considered the flag so important that he personally wrote to Vice-Admiral Sir Gerald Gladstone, Commander-in-Chief Far-Eastern Station, to enlist his help. This started an endeavour which was to last almost six years, the course of which can more easily be followed from the actual correspondence which ensued.

First Sea Lord, Admiralty, London, SW1

15 January 1958

Dear Revd Wild,

Thank you for your letter of 9 January 1958, which I found on my return from Sandringham.

I remember your brother coming to me with the Union Jack used at the surrender of Singapore to the Japanese and which, by some miraculous means, he had been able to retain hidden, even in the face of Japanese brutality in trying to discover its whereabouts.

I readily agreed to his suggestion that it should be hoisted on the day that the Japanese surrendered to us; and with his concurrence I subsequently presented it to Singapore.

I do not know what the present position is about the Flag but I am, today, sending a letter to the Commander-in-Chief Far-East, asking him to find out. I enclose a copy of this letter and will let you know the answer in due course.

Yours sincerely,

Mountbatten of Burma

– – –

COPY

From: First Sea Lord

To: Vice-Admiral Sir Gerald Gladstone, KCB, Commander-in-Chief Far-East Station, HMS *Newfoundland*.

Newspapers report that the Union Jack which I presented to Singapore has been removed from the Council Chamber by the new Mayor. This evidently refers to the Union Jack which was retained by Colonel Wild and hidden in Changi during the Japanese Occupation. On the Japanese surrender he handed the Flag to me and it was re-hoisted ceremoniously and then given to Singapore.

Colonel Wild was unfortunately killed in a flying accident at Hong Kong a few months later, but his brother, The Reverend R.D.F. Wild, Housemaster at Eton, has written asking whether it would be possible to recover this Union Jack to be retained in his family.

I would be grateful if you could go into this matter and see whether, in fact, the Union Jack is to be 'thrown out' by the Singapore Council, in which case I would like to get hold of it and give it to Colonel Wild's brother, or whether, in fact, it is intended that the Flag should be kept in some honourable position in Singapore in view of its historic association with the courageous behaviour of our prisoners-of-war in Changi.

Lord Louis had a reply from Sir Gerald Gladstone almost immediately, and sent a copy of it to David.

First Sea Lord, Admiralty, London, SW1

28 January 1958

Dear Revd Wild,

With reference to my letter of 15 January 1958, I have now heard from the Commander-in-Chief Far-East, and I think his letter is of sufficient interest for me to send you a copy. In these circumstances I hope you will agree that we ought to leave matters as they are for the time being.

Yours sincerely,

Mountbatten of Burma

–   –   –

COPY

From: Vice-Admiral Sir Gerald Gladstone, KCB

To: Admiral of the Fleet, The Earl Mountbatten of Burma, KG

My Dear First Sea Lord,

Thank you for your letter of 15 January 1958.

The newspaper reports and your assumptions are roughly correct: The Mace was also removed by the new very left-wing Mayor. They are now deposited in the City Hall strong room.

Before making the request you suggest, on your behalf, (which I think would very likely be refused now anyway as has already a somewhat similar one for the Mace) I would like you to consider whether your proposal is really in our best interests and that of the cold war here. So long as Wild's Union Jack is here in the Council's possession it remains, with the Mace, a symbol to many of freedom and friendliness to Britain: and there are a lot of people here who are very dismayed at the Mayor's action, who have strong feelings about it, and who would be terribly disheartened if the Flag left Singapore.

Now in the strong room, later it may (even with this Mayor) emerge on show in a case. A Mayor of a different political colour may restore it, and the Mace which is still a subject of local controversy, to its old position. But not if the Wild family have it back in England.

For my part, I have every sympathy with the family and would like them to have it in any case. The courage of the prisoners-of-war is a part of history which no Mayor will shake: but the Flag was a personal relic of a single man.

However, at this moment the Flag is more a piece of politics than of history: it is quite safe, but if the Wild family want it back it will take some time for the climate to be suitable for the request you suggest.

I have, of course, discussed this with the Governor who shares my views expressed in this letter.

Yours sincerely,

signed: Gerald Gladstone

Lord Mountbatten's opinion that they should let the matter rest would perhaps have deterred lesser men from pressing further for the return of the flag, but not so David Wild, who showed the same determination as his brother. Field-Marshal Sir Gerald Templer, whose son was in

David's house at Eton, started the ball rolling again almost three years later, in December 1960, by getting in touch with Lord Selkirk, the UK Commissioner-General for South-East Asia. Templer promised David he would make every endeavour to trace the flag, as he was about to visit Singapore on business. Eventually, it was confirmed that the flag was still at City Hall, and the following letters show the train of events for the next three years:

Field-Marshal Sir Gerald Templer, 12 Wilton Street, London, SW1

10 March 1961

My Dear David,

I enclose a copy of a letter which I have had from Geordie Selkirk, the UK Commissioner-General for South-East Asia, on the subject of the Union Jack. I do not know where we go from here. I have written back to ask him to have another thorough search made.

Yours ever,

Gerald

— — —

COPY

From: The United Kingdom Commissioner-General for South-East Asia, Phoenix Park, Singapore.

To: Field-Marshal Sir Gerald Templer, GCB, GCMG, KBE, DSO

Dear Gerald,

I had a word with Lee Kuan Yew a couple of days ago with regard to the Union Jack which was in Changi Prison Camp during the war. He affirmed resolutely that it was in the Singapore Museum... In fact, it is impossible to know what is in the Museum at all. When I made my request Lee said that he had no objection to my making a thorough search, which I will endeavour to do.

I think there is probably at least something in what the Prime Minister is saying, but if the Museum is in such a mess, I find it a little difficult to know why he is so sure that the Union Jack is there.

I do hope you both recovered from your exhausting journey in these parts.

signed: Geordie (Selkirk)

Two and a half years later David heard again from Field-Marshal Sir Gerald Templer:

12 Wilton Street,
London, SW1

31 December 1963

My dear David,

I send you a copy of a letter which I have had from the Assistant High Commissioner in Singapore, together with a copy of my reply.

I have also rung Golds in the Commonwealth Relations Office saying that I feel strongly that the 'Wild Union Jack' must go to Charterhouse. I will let you know what happens when I hear some more.

Anyway, you'll be pleased, I know. It's taken three years to track it down.

Yours ever,

Gerald

– – –

COPY

From: P. B. C. Moore, Assistant High Commissioner, British High Commission, Union Building, Collyer Quay, Singapore.

Dear Field-Marshal Templer,

You will remember that you had some correspondence with Lord Selkirk about the Union Jack which was carried by General Percival (*sic* Brig. Torrance) at the surrender to the Japanese in 1942, was kept in Changi during the occupation by Major Wild, and at the liberation was given by Wild to Admiral Mountbatten, who subsequently handed it over to the Singapore authorities. I am glad to say that after pursuing various clues, we have now discovered the flag in a most unlikely looking box in the City Hall. We were put on to this by Middleton-Smith, now Bursar at Cheltenham, who was formerly the official in charge of the City Council. There was also in the box a second Union Jack brought in by the liberating forces in 1945. These were the two flags which hung in the City Hall until they were taken down by Ong Eng Guan when he became Mayor at the end of 1957. I subsequently spoke to Lee Kuan Yew about the flags, and he agreed that we might have them. They now rest in my office.

I have written to Tony Golds, Head of the Far-East and Pacific Department in the Commonwealth Relations Office, suggesting that the flags should be handed over to the Imperial War Museum, on the understanding that if at any time in the future the Singapore or Malaysian Government of the day expressed the desire to have the flags back, they would be returned to Singapore. I hope you will think this is a good idea. I expect Tony Golds will be getting into touch with you.

Is there any chance of seeing you in Singapore again? My wife and I both send our warmest good wishes to Lady Templer and yourself.

Yours sincerely,

signed: Philip Moore

— — —

COPY

From: Field-Marshal Sir Gerald Templer

To: P.B.C. Moore, Assistant High Commissoner

Many thanks for your letter of 24 December about the Union Jacks. Needless to say, I was delighted to receive it.

I will get in touch with Golds in the Commonwealth Relations Office, but in the meantime, I want to get a short letter off to you on the subject of the eventual destination of the flags.

I started this correspondence with Lord Selkirk in December 1960. I did so because I wanted to track down the 'Wild Union Jack' as his old school – Charterhouse – hoped very much that they would be able to find it and display it in their Great Hall, since Wild, long since dead, is a considerable hero to boys of present generations. This seemed to me a most estimable purpose, and I would think it would have a much bigger effect in the Great Hall at Charterhouse rather than as just one more exhibit in the Imperial War Museum.

I have no means of saying, but I would imagine that Charterhouse would accept it on loan, so to speak, and with the condition which you suggest in the last paragraph of your letter.

This was great news! At last the flag was traced and permission granted for it to leave Singapore; the problem now was to get it home.

It so happened that the father of another boy in David's house at Eton was a Queen's Messenger, and he volunteered to bring the Union Jack back to England in the Diplomatic Bag. What an excellent method of transport this would have been, but Lee Kuan Yew had other ideas and considered it should be entrusted only to the Royal Navy. On the day of its expected arrival David telephoned the Imperial War Museum to check that it was, at last, safely in their custody. No, there was no sign of it, and eventually it transpired that the Royal Navy had dumped the flag, in its box, on the quayside at Portsmouth, where it was left unattended for some considerable time.

It was Patrick Wild who approached the Imperial War Museum to ask if they would loan the Union Jack to their old school, Charterhouse, to which suggestion they readily agreed. Patrick and David, with the

Headmaster, Mr. Oliver Van Oss, performed the dedication ceremony in Charterhouse school chapel in July 1967. The flag now hangs in the ante-chapel with an inscription, affixed to the wall below, written by Oliver Van Oss, Headmaster from 1965 to 1973:

> This flag bore witness to one of the blackest defeats in British Military History. It was carried by Colonel C. H. D. Wild (OC) at the capitulation of Singapore to the Japanese on 15 February 1942. Afterwards, at considerable personal risk, he acquired the flag and took it with him when imprisoned in the notorious Changi Gaol. There he and other prisoners courageously managed to conceal it from their captors for three and a half years. On 12 September 1945 the Supreme Allied Commander South-East Asia invited Colonel Wild to hoist this same flag over the surrender of the Japanese forces. And so the wheel came full circle. Colonel Wild (R 1921 – 1927) was tragically killed in an air disaster and his flag was laid in Charterhouse Chapel by his brothers as a memorial to him and a memento of the two historic moments to which he and the flag had borne witness.
>
> *Domus non immemor*

BIBLIOGRAPHY

The Heroes, Ronald McKie.

Destined Meeting, Leslie Bell.

Towards the Setting Sun, James Bradley.

The Thai-Burma Railway, article for *World War Investigator*, Ewart Escritt.

Alarm Starboard, Geoffrey Brooke.

Lectures by Lt-Gen. Heath on the Malayan Campaign, given to officers at Changi in 1942.

Mountbatten – The Official Biography, Philip Ziegler.

Article in *The Times*, October 1945,Ian Morrison.

Expedition to Singkep, article in *Blackwood's Magazine*, Cyril Wild.

Verbatim transcripts of the Tokyo War Crimes Trials, in the possession of the Imperial War Museum, by kind permission of Roderick Suddaby and Philip Reed.

An Overview of the Historical Importance of the Tokyo War Trial, John Pritchard.

The Other Nuremberg: The Untold Story of the Tokyo War Crime Trials, Arnold C. Brackman

INDEX